Sacred Chaos

Bruce A. Green
Denver, CO

Sacred Chaos
and
the Quest for
Spiritual
Intimacy

JAMES R. NEWBY

CONTINUUM · NEW YORK

1998

The Continuum Publishing Company
370 Lexington Avenue
New York, NY 10017

Printed in the United States of America

Library of Congress Cataloging-in-Publication Data

Newby, James R.
    Sacred chaos and the quest for spiritual intimacy / by James
R. Newby.
    ISBN 0-8264-1080-4
    1. Newby, James R. 2. Spiritual biography — United States.
3. Quakers — United States — Biography. 4. Spiritual life —
Society of Friends.   I. Title.
BX7795.N435A3   1998
289.8'092 — dc21
    [B]   97-38954
                                                        CIP

Love has nothing to do with order.

— COLUMBANUS

To
Mark and Karla, Judith, Melanie, Nancy,
Kay, Melissa, Lawrence and Jenny,
my spiritual partners in chaos . . .

To
Sherry, my spiritual counselor . . .

And To
Elizabeth and Alicia Marie,
my family,
who love me because of . . .
and in spite of . . .

*The search for spirit, for God, is
ultimately the quest to know ourselves
in our heights and depths. It is the task
of Everyman and woman and of every
heroic journey to go beyond our
certitudes and doubts, beyond our sure
knowledge and understanding, in the
direction of an ever-unfolding truth.
It was, is, and always will be the
greatest human adventure . . .*

— SAM KEEN

Hymns to an Unknown God

Contents

ACKNOWLEDGMENTS

I have never been able to write in isolation, and this is certainly true of this volume. I am grateful to many—my former colleagues at the Earlham School of Religion in Indiana, and especially to Peter Anderson, my colleague in writing who introduced me to Continuum; First Friends Meeting in Greensboro, North Carolina; North Carolina Yearly Meeting of Friends; the staff and members of Plymouth Congregational Church in Des Moines, Iowa; and all of my friends at Ham's (You know who you are!). These are my faith communities, wherein most of the ideas expressed here were first shared. I thank Karole Cox, my administrative assistant at the D. Elton Trueblood Yokefellow Academy for Applied Christianity, for her care and willingness to accept more responsibility as I continued to write. Floyd Thatcher, friend and editor, was most helpful as he suggested improvements to the manuscript. For their supportive love and concern, I express my gratitude to my brother John, sister-in-law Shelley, and sister Darlene . . . *I love you dearly.*

Finally, I am grateful to my close spiritual friends and family, in whom I confided and trusted my feelings of chaos. It is to them that I dedicate this book, for without their encouragement, patience, and love, I would not have been able to begin, much less complete this project.

Mutely I rise amid tears
Uncomprehending but called
To step toward the chaos
Where lies the only possibility
For life . . .
— RUTH NAYLOR

PROLOGUE

Everything Is Going to Be All Right

*I say to you: one must have chaos in oneself
in order to give birth to a dancing star.*
— FRIEDRICH NIETZSCHE

My dear friend and mentor had died in December, and my marriage of twenty-five years seemed to be at an end. In an effort to complete two book projects, I was spending the month of February on the coast of North Carolina. The burdens on my heart were overwhelming, and although I was still functional, I was feeling lonely and depressed. Beginning with the death of my father in 1985, life had become a litany of loss. While I was away for this month, my primary motivation to get out of bed in the morning was the anticipation that I would see the sun rise over the beautiful Atlantic Ocean. And so, on this tenth day of my self-imposed exile at the coast, I awakened to the smell of coffee brewing and proceeded to dress in my running suit for what had become my ritual walk to the beach.

The condominium in which I was staying was not more than seventy-five yards from the water. The sun was already casting a pink glow across the horizon, and the ocean waves were rhythmically pounding the shore. It was cold that morning, perhaps in the mid-thirties. Everything seemed crisp and alive. I stared off into the vastness of the sea and began to weep. I lamented where my forty-five years on this earth had brought me. Many years worth of repressed pain flowed up from the pit of my stomach, manifesting in a torrent of tears. Hiding my face behind my cup of hot coffee, I sat down in the sand.

What occurred next is difficult to describe. As clear as if someone were seated next to me, I heard the words, "Everything is going to be all right." I was startled, and began to glance from side to side, looking for the source of what I had just heard. Again, "Everything is going to be all right." There was no other physical presence on the beach—just me, my cup, and the surf.

I stood up, took my last gulp of coffee, and began to walk the narrow sand-filled path back to my February home. The words, from wherever they had come, brought a strange sense of comfort to my depressing circumstances. "Everything is going to be all right." I was beginning to sense that my chaos had just been tinged with the sacred. The words provided a lining of hope at one of my neediest hours. It was a profoundly spiritual experience—an experience that one *feels*, and which can only be fully understood by those who have known similar experiences. I believe that the Infinite had reached out to me, the finite, on a lonely North Carolina beach, and I have not been the same since.

Pain and loss produce chaos. Chaos can have gentle beginnings, such as an inner tug deep within our souls that awakens us to the realization that the life we are now living is not fulfilling. Chaos can also begin in more dramatic ways— the death of a loved one, divorce, the loss of a job, or academic failure. Whatever the impetus, chaos is uncomfortable. It moves us out of familiar patterns and known ways; causes us to re-evaluate what is important, how our lives are being lived; and, if we heed the signs, sets us on a journey of seeking *more* of what is missing.

The consequences of such chaos can be devastating to all around us. We each have a circle of friends and family who *know* us in certain ways. They become comfortable in their expectations of how we will respond to them and to the issues of life. As the chaos grows within, this circle can become confused and thrown out of the familiar orbit to which they have become accustomed. Fearing disruption of the family, friendships, position in the community, many of us will "fake it" for a while to maintain peace. Most of us do not want our chaos to be disruptive. And so, for the sake of the "children," or "family peace," or "financial security," we will try to keep the chaos in check, repressing what can only be described as the irrepressible spiritual hunger that one is feeling. This we do to our spiritual detriment.

Chaos becomes sacred when it moves us in ever more powerful ways, to more consciously be about the greatest of human adventures: the quest for spiritual intimacy. In truth, *all* of life is a quest for spiritual intimacy. We can deny it or embrace it; what we cannot do is *ignore* it. Chaos intensifies the quest. We are spiritual beings in search of connection. This is a universal truth. But each of us is also a unique story which is continuously unfolding as the search progresses. In the mythology of Genesis we are created out of chaos, and it is out of the chaos in our lives that we are re-created over and over again as we seek spiritual intimacy. It is a continuous cycle of God and us, co-creating new beings, out of which we give birth to dancing stars.

The image of life as a journey which creatively unfolds minute by minute and day by day has always been intriguing to me. In this regard I am not alone among baby boomers, for journey theology is a most important concept to my generation. John Bunyan's *Pilgrim's Progress* is the best example of this process in classic Christian literature, but it is a thematic undercurrent in many other works as well.

Each of us is the essence of plot. *This book is about my personal pilgrimage, sharing the plot which God and I have created together out of chaos, weaving it into the tapestry of the larger human/spiritual story. Hopefully, it will be a map for others as they make their own way through chaos.* In this way my life, as with all lives, is paradoxically, *uniquely universal.*

Whatever else we thought the meaning of life was before we encountered chaos, we now know something different as the quest for spiritual intimacy becomes primary. What we used to make fun of, we will find ourselves doing, and what we used to do, we will now walk away from. Such a quest will take us through many passages of growth, but it will most surely encompass the five outlined here—*Recovering Passion; Processing Pain; Exploring Prayer; Dancing with Paradox;* and *Experiencing Pilgrimage.* These passages are not placed before us in a linear fashion, whereby we pass from one into another, clearly and distinctly. Instead, they are circuitous, weaving around, in and through us as we grow into greater spiritual intimacy. We process pain while at the same time we are recovering passion and dancing with paradox. We experience pilgrimage while we process pain and explore prayer. We explore prayer while at the same time we dance with paradox and recover passion . . . and on and on it goes, as we constantly weave our way through chaos to ever deeper spiritual intimacy. All experiences in life are the result of the coming together of a multiplicity of factors. And it is certainly so with *spiritual experience.*

Finally, out of the experience of chaos our hearts will open to the exciting possibility of giving birth to a dancing star. This quest is really a journey of the heart. "Now here is my secret; a very simple secret, indeed," we read in *The Little Prince*, "it is only with the heart that one can see rightly." In the words of Blaise Pascal, "The heart has reasons that the mind knows not of." Open your heart. Follow your heart. Seek the reasons of the heart which will propel you on your quest, and which will help you give birth to your own, very special, dancing star. In the end, this dancing star will light your way to ever deepening spiritual intimacy, and to the important truth that everything will, indeed, be all right.

James R. Newby
Newbeginnings
Oriental, North Carolina

1

Recovering Passion

To be awake is to be alive.
— HENRY DAVID THOREAU

I didn't recognize him at first. He was bent over, head down, and eyes fixed on each short step he was taking. "Johnnie, is that you?" I had not seen Johnnie since last October when he had done some yard work for me. This was mid-January. Recognizing my voice, he stopped to look up, and as our eyes met his woundedness became fully exposed. I could hardly bear to look him in the eye. "Johnnie, are you all right?" "Oh, James, I have been put through the medical ringer." Each word was said haltingly and painfully. "Since I saw you last I have had a serious heart attack. The doctor has told me that the damage is so great that I can never mow another lawn."

Devastating news for a man who loved yard work. For Johnnie it was more than just a job, it was a *passion*. I have never known a person who knew more about different types of lawn mowers and the various kinds of grass than Johnnie. From the moment I would pick him up (he didn't drive) until the time we reached my home on the other side of town, he would recite a litany of grass and mowers. He lived for the spring and summer when he could be outdoors.

"I can never mow another lawn." The words just hung there between us as he talked about how he had almost died and his new set of limitations. I listened for about ten minutes, hugged him, and told him I would stay in touch. He turned and continued his slow and painful walk to wherever he was going. I turned and went about my business, but he has stayed on my mind and heart.

Johnnie is a parable for many in our time. Head down, bent over, and eyes fixed on each short step, we reluctantly trudge through the patterns of our well-worn lives, devoid of passion and meaning. What is life without a sense of meaning and a passion which gives it vitality? *Mere existence.*

At our best, human beings *want* more than mere existence and *need* more than mere existence. We are meaning-seeking, social creatures. Two of the most basic longings in life are to find purpose in one's existence, and to be in relationship with one another. Both of these longings are intertwined, for meaning in life can be found in our relationships with others, and the most satisfying relationships can be instrumental in the search for meaning in life.

At this particular time in human history, this search for meaning and relationship has become intensified. In a time of accelerated change, like we are in now, there is a corresponding need to clarify meaning *and* to know that we are not alone. In this dual quest, *passion* can be an important vehicle in driving the search. It helps to push us beyond the worn-out patterns and dead-ends of the past, and moves us to venture into a new spiritual landscape.

Thomas Moore is a psychologist who lived as a monk in a Catholic religious order for twelve years. He has degrees in both psychology and theology, a powerful combination in today's world where there is currently the intense search for the two basic longings of meaning and relationship. Moore has written a best-selling book titled *Care of the Soul*. A few years ago I asked him how he accounted for the book's amazing success. He said, "I ask that question all over the country, and what people tell me is that they are hungry for something deeper than what they usually get. . . . People are ready and willing to explore things without being given simple answers."

There certainly are no "simple answers" to the quest for meaning and spiritual interconnectedness with one another. In a world which seems, at times, preoccupied by the superficial, and where a microwave theology produces theological "McNuggets," we can understand the "hunger for something deeper." To care for the soul (the dictionary defines *soul* as "the essential part"), i.e., find meaning and interconnectedness, we must first acknowledge the feeling of emptiness in the very core of our being, and the bankruptcy of conventional psychotherapy and social science to feed such emptiness.

• • •

FINDING CONNECTION IN A DISCONNECTED WORLD

Only connect.

— E. M. FORSTER

My soul has made a start on finding the passion it seeks when I have connected with others in the creation of community. A friend telephoned the other day and said, "I am tired of being a 'Lone-Ranger' in my ministry. I need to form a community of support." I agree. As a Quaker/Christian, I have equated the formation of such community with the spiritual underpinnings of these traditions. One can certainly recover meaning and passion within other communal traditions, but for my purposes here, I can only share out of my own experience, writing out of the center which has helped to form me.

We know that we can be creative alone, but when we can share our faith, dreams, and vision with like-minded and like-hearted soul mates, the creativity is enhanced and the passion for such creativity is revived. We can worship God alone, but when we worship in a community of like-minded and like-hearted seekers, the worship experience goes *deeper*. Few words are more meaningful to Christians than "one another." Indeed, if there is one continuous theme which runs throughout the entire New Testament of the Bible, it is the theme that we are "members one of another."

Many scholars believe that First Thessalonians is the earliest book or letter written to be included in the New Testament. In this brief letter to the Church at Thessalonica, the Apostle Paul uses the words "one another" six separate times: "May the Lord make you increase and abound in love to *one another*" (3:12), "For you yourselves have been taught by God to love *one another*" (4:9), "Therefore comfort *one another*" (4:18), "Therefore encourage *one another* and build *one another* up" (5:11), "Always seek to do good to *one another* and to all" (5:15).

The creation of "one another" communities, where meaning can be sought and passion can be recovered, will take many and varied forms, but there are certain elements which are helpful in any formation process. First of all, community is created when we gather together—two, three, or five hundred, and *experience the transforming, life-changing power of a Spirit beyond our finitude*. A beautiful example of this transforming experience is found in the Book of Acts 4:31–32: "And when they had prayed, the place in which they were gathered was shaken; and they were all filled with the Holy Spirit and spoke the word of God with boldness. Now the company of those who believed were of one heart and soul." Being *shaken* by an experience of the Living God while "gathered together" leads to the expression of love for one another, becoming "one heart and soul" in beloved community.

Another element in the formation of community has to do with the tradition of stories. When we *tell and retell the stories of the meaningful experiences shared, we gather together our memories*. We re-member in community, as opposed to dismember. The stories keep the fire of fellowship ablaze. In the Gospel of Luke, chapter 24, the disciples remember and tell the story of how their master walked with them on the Emmaus Road, and in verse 32 exclaim, "Did not our hearts burn within us while he talked to us on the road, while he opened to us the scriptures?" Remembering helped the disciples to form community via shared experience. We are held together by the repetition of such meaningful experiences within our traditions.

A third mark of community formation has to do with the *processing of one another's pain and becoming a part of the fellowship of suffering*. In the words of the Apostle Paul, "If one member suffers, all suffer together" (1 Cor. 12:36). When in community, the pain we each carry can be shared, and as Albert Schweitzer has written, such experiences of pain can lead to a new place of interconnectedness: "He who has been delivered from pain must not think he is now free again, and at liberty to take life up just as it was before, entirely forgetful of the past. He is now a person 'whose eyes are open' with regard to pain and anguish, and he must help . . . to bring to others deliverance which he himself enjoyed."

Community is also created when we *encourage one another by practicing the discipline of encouragement*. The central biblical text for this injunction comes from 1 Thess. 5:11: "Therefore encourage one another and build one another up." We live in a very critical and impatient time, when finding fault comes easily. Life is hard enough without the added burden of a critical spirit that would tear down, rather than build up one another.

Finally, community is formed when we *become sensitive never to wound the hearts of others*. The Apostle Paul writes, "Let all bitterness and wrath and anger and clamor and slander be put away from you, with all malice, and be kind to one another, tenderhearted, forgiving one another, as God in Christ forgave you" (Eph. 4:31–32). Hateful words can be devastating. Cold stares can diminish another person to a mere object. A circle can be drawn to exclude people from our own in-group, and we can totally ignore persons who are crying out for friendship because they do not quite measure up to our standards. We know how to wound hearts.

Zorba the Greek tells of an old neighbor he knew as a child:

> One day he took me on his knee and placed his hand on my hand as though he were giving me his blessing. "Alexis," he said, "I'm going to tell you a secret. You're too small to understand now, but you'll understand when you are bigger. Listen, little one: Neither the seven stories of heaven nor the seven stories of earth are enough to contain God; but a person's heart can contain Him. So be very careful, Alexis—and may my blessing go with you—never to wound a person's heart."
> (*Zorba the Greek*)

Being in community is hard work because relationships are hard work. We yearn to be in relationship. Therefore, we must learn to love the difficult. When we come together through a transformative experience with the Infinite, telling the stories of the meaningful experiences shared within the beloved community, processing one another's pain, and becoming a part of the fellowship of suffering, practicing the ministry of encouragement, and being sensitive never to wound the hearts of others, we can at least begin the task of creating centers of loving fellowship, which, in turn, can help us recover passion, and, consequently, change the world.

• • •

SPIRITUAL FRIENDSHIP

Our relationships are laboratories
for our spiritual growth and awakening.
— MOLLY YOUNG BROWN

Although the creation of a beloved community, and living as a part of such community is helpful for the recovery of passion and the quest for spiritual intimacy, it does not negate the importance of discovering at least *one* person who can be a true spiritual friend. To take the risk and openly share a spiritual kinship with another person places one in a vulnerable position. And yet this vulnerability is worth the risk if it keeps the passion for life ever vibrant, and the meaning of such life ever before us. Our souls yearn for more than physical presence or humorous anecdotes. We need more than a lunch partner or a colleague who will never share more than amusing political or social commentary. We want a friendship that is without pretense, and without the fear of expressing deep emotion. This is a friendship centered in a spiritual union of souls wherein nothing is considered too personal, too sacred, too outrageous, or too emotionally disturbing to be shared together.

The movie *Dances with Wolves* was a very important picture for me. At the climactic point in the movie, we hear these words: "Dances-with-Wolves, do you know that I am your friend?! Do you know that I will *always* be your friend?!" The words are spoken by Wind-in-His-Hair, passionately expressed from a cliff overlooking a small Sioux encampment. Dances-with-Wolves, formerly Lt. Dunbar, and played by the actor

Kevin Costner, is preparing to separate himself from his adopted Sioux tribe because his continued presence in his Native American community endangers them all. The U.S. Army has labeled him a traitor, and they are looking for him.

Knowing that he would never see his friend again; searching for a way to express his love, and struggling to share his innermost feelings, Wind-in-His-Hair asks a question, and at the same time makes a powerful statement—"Do you know that I am your friend?"

The quest for spiritual intimacy is fueled by vulnerability. The more open and vulnerable we become in relationship, the more passion is generated.

James Kavanaugh has written a poem titled, "Will You Be My Friend?" In the penetrating and vulnerable style for which he is known, Kavanaugh writes, in part:

> Will you be my friend?
> There are so many reasons why you never should:
> I'm sometimes sullen, often shy, acutely sensitive,
> My fear erupts as anger. I find it hard to give,
> I talk about myself when I'm afraid
> And often spend a day without anything to say.
>> But I will make you laugh
>> And love you quite a bit
>> And hold you when you're sad.
> I cry a little almost every day
> Because I'm more caring than the strangers ever know,
> And, if at times, I show my tender side
> (The soft and warmer part I hide)
>> I wonder,
>> Will you be my friend?
> A friend
>> Who far beyond the feebleness of any vow or tie
>> Will touch the secret place where I am really I,

To know the pain of lips that plead and eyes that weep,
Who will not run away when you find me in the street
Alone and lying mangled by my quota of defeats
But will stop and stay—to tell me of another day
When I was beautiful.
Will you be my friend?

Will you be my friend? It is a question which reaches into the heart of what it means to be human. Who of us doesn't want someone to make us *laugh* and *love* us quite a bit, and *hold* us when we are sad? We not only want interconnectedness, but a connection wherein we can be *intimately vulnerable*.

The basis for this kind of conjunction in human relationship is *trust*. To be a spiritual friend with someone who will make us laugh and who will love us and hold us when sad, implies that at the core of such friendship is a strong and mutual *trust*. "Trust is the basis of any relationship," writes Craig Nakken, "If a relationship is not based on trust, the relationship becomes a struggle. . . . Trust allows us the ability to heal and the freedom to connect with others" (*The Addictive Personality*). Jesus said, "I have called you friends for all that I have heard from my father I have made known to you" (John 15:15). Jesus *revealed* himself to his friends. He became vulnerable with them, sharing all that he had heard from God. He *trusted* his disciples, and they became his friends.

The issue of trust is centered in several episodes of the comic strip *Peanuts*, featuring Charlie Brown, Lucy, and a football. In one *Peanuts* episode, Charlie is quite certain about the fact that an offer from Lucy to hold the ball for him to kick will end as all the other attempts have. She'll pull the ball away just as he is ready to kick it and he'll end up flat on his back.

He says to her: "You must think I'm crazy. You say you'll hold the ball, but you won't. You'll pull it away and I'll break my neck."

With the look of an angel, Lucy responds: "Why, Charlie Brown, how you talk! I wouldn't think of such a thing. I'm a changed person. Look, isn't this a face you can trust?"

Since Charlie Brown is Charlie Brown, he accepts Lucy at her word. "All right, you hold the ball and I'll come running up and kick it."

Sure enough, the expected happens and, as he flies through the air to smash to the ground, he can only shout: "She did it again!"

In the last scene, Lucy leans over Charlie to say: "I admire you, Charlie Brown. You have such faith in human nature."

Trusting one another in a spiritual friendship takes courage. We are vulnerable when we trust. We could get hurt. The ball could be snatched away and we could fall to the ground. And yet there are things worse than getting hurt, and that is to close oneself off from a passion-reviving, spiritual friendship because we fear trusting. The quest for spiritual intimacy, wherein we find meaning in our chaos and recover passion, means that we will carry some Charlie Brown in us, trusting that the world, as a whole, and our friends in particular, provide safe places.

James Kavanaugh asks a universal question: "Will you be my friend?" It is a courageous question, especially when we have been hurt, and when trust has been eroded. By risking the possibility of hurt in relationship, hour by hour and day by day, *trusting*, even when we have no reason to trust, bears testimony to our human need for interconnectedness. And spiritual friends make such connection a holy sacrament.

* * *

FINDING ONESELF OUTSIDE ONESELF

We learn who we are
in the very process of not thinking about who we are.
— KAREN CASEY

"Can I buy you a beer?" It was John asking the question as he climbed onto the bar stool next to me. I didn't know his last name. We had become acquainted one evening at our neighborhood pub. "Sure, John," I responded, "How are you?" "Not well, Jim. This is a bad day for me." His face reflected his depressed mood. Resting his cheeks on his hands, he stared straight ahead, and a heaviness welled up in his eyes. "Do you want to talk about it?," I asked. Turning toward me, John inquired, "Jim, you're a religious type, aren't you?" "I have dabbled in it," I said, half smiling. "Well, this is the first anniversary of the death of my son, and I am on my way home to be met by a wife who will be crying, and I don't know what to do. I thought you might be able to help."

I listened as John slowly and painfully told me the story about his son who had died as an infant. He shared about all of the expectations that he and his wife had had for this child, and all of the excitement they had shared, only to have it taken away a few weeks after birth. John was still not certain *how* the child had died, only that it had something to do with a malfunctioning heart.

John needed to talk, and he felt that I could be one who would listen to him and understand his sorrow, as well as help him to respond in a positive way toward his grief-stricken wife. After about an hour and three beers, John and I left to go our separate ways. I went over the hill to dinner at my apartment, and he went down the hill to grieve with his wife.

Recovering passion in one's life can be a multifaceted process. Connecting with a community of like-minded believers, as well as to connect with one or two spiritual friends in whom we can trust with our story, are two parts of the path toward such passion recovery. It can also be helpful to go beyond our normal cultural context, interacting with people outside of our usual circle of operation. The neighborhood pub is such a context for me. Here I meet persons, experiencing all levels of broken humanity, and I can interact with them in a "safe" place. Beyond the stories of sports and business ventures, which often serve as a veneer for their pain, the people who come to this pub are hurting, seeking connection, and looking for others who will hear their stories, and not be condemned for their human failures.

George Macleod, founder of the Iona Fellowship, has written some poignant words reminding us of the cultural context in which Jesus was crucified:

> I simply argue that the cross should be raised at the center of the marketplace as well as on the steeple of the church. I am recovering the claim that Jesus was not crucified in a cathedral between two candles, but on a cross between two thieves; on the town's garbage heap; at a crossroad, so cosmopolitan they had to write his title in Hebrew and Latin and Greek . . . at the kind of place where cynics talk smut, and thieves curse, and soldiers gamble. Because that is where he died. And that is what he died for. And that is what he died about. That is where Christians ought to be and what Christians ought to be about. (*Quaker Life*, March, 1991)

For those of us who have grown up within the culture of the Christian faith, and who have lived out this faith within the confines of a particular denomination or sect, the "pub"or "marketplace" can be a scary place. It moves one into an environment beyond the safety of the stained glass windows, and into a cosmopolitan world where few Christian types have dared to venture. In the chaos we feel, a change of scenery helps contribute to the recovery of passion, as well as an attitude of *trust*, trusting that God can be found, and perhaps more easily found, in the context of the local pub or marketplace as well as what are considered more "holy" settings.

On a larger scale, to go beyond the island of wealth known as North America can be passion recovering as well. We do not have to travel very far to realize the sterility of our environment and how the trappings of wealth keep us isolated from the other three-fourths of the world. A trip across the border to Mexico, or a brief airplane ride to Belize or Haiti, will open our spiritual eyes to conditions that are difficult to imagine anyone living in. Open sewers, the stench from which will never leave you, run throughout Belize City, Mexico City, and Port au Prince, with children half naked, playing along these canals, spreading disease and hopelessness. Walking these streets, looking into the eyes of the residents, smelling all of the different odors that make up such a culture, having children beg from you, from the moment you step onto the street, until you go back to your hotel or place of residence, is to begin to find yourself outside of yourself.

One early December a few years ago, the entire faculty of the Earlham School of Religion traveled to Belize. We spent a week in what we called "a multicultural experience," traveling around the country, touching the lives of those with whom we came in contact, and being touched by all who interacted with us. Upon arrival back in the United States, I found it difficult to adjust. I distinctly remember one incident which caused me particular distress. It was the week before Christmas, and I was speaking in a church just a few days after my return. Immediately before I was to bring the message, the bell choir of this church performed a number of traditional Christmas songs. Each of the bell ringers wore white gloves and matching outfits. The bells were all brass and polished to shine as they were rung. As I listened to this mini bell concert, it was all that I could do to stay seated and not walk out. Now, I love music and bell choirs, especially at Christmas. But the contrast between what I had experienced in the Christianity of poverty-stricken Belize and what I was then experiencing in the sterility of North American Christianity was almost *unbearable*. Deep down in the recesses of my heart, I felt God moving within me, transforming me to find myself, outside of myself, and my culture.

I have not been able to forget what I had experienced in Belize, or what I see each time I visit Mexico. But one does not have to leave the country to know the spiritually distressing dichotomy of rich and poor. I was visiting a friend in Washington, D.C., a few months ago, who worked at that time as an assistant attorney general in the Justice Department. Walking around the outside of this huge complex which houses the legal system of the federal government, I couldn't help but notice a man, obviously one of America's homeless, sleeping on a heating grate under the sign "Justice Department." It made for a most ironic picture, in this, the wealthiest nation on earth.

Recently I was having lunch at a Woolworth's lunch counter, where I "connected" with the waitress. For me, it was an "out of culture" experience, and another spiritual example of how we find ourselves outside of ourselves. I was awakened to her presence from behind the pages of my book, when I heard her say, "I ain't got none of that there pie left, but I can get you a good piece of pumpkin." She was speaking to a customer down the line from me. Looking to be near sixty-five years old, she hopped from position to position with a grin on her face and a bounce in her step that would put younger women (and men) to shame. "Charlie, are you still dating that pretty little thing you had in here the other day? How does she stand you?" It was nonstop verbal assault from one customer to another, and they loved it. "Can I get you anything else? Not that you need it, but I was told that I had to ask!"

As I watched her carrying out orders, responding to the cook's bell like one of Pavlov's dogs, and witnessed the cheerful demeanor with which she approached her work, I wondered. I wondered what kind of life she lives away from the lunch counter. I wondered if she had a family—is she a mother and wife? As I studied the lines in her face and the gray hair she did not try to hide behind a bottle of Clairol, I wondered if she ever pondered the very human questions of, "Why are we here?" and "Why do we die?" and "What is it that makes life worth living?" Has she ever considered the eternal significance of her work— the serving of yesterday's meat loaf covered with gravy as today's luncheon special?

Her grammar was as poor as I have ever heard. Earlier in life I would have flippantly labeled her a simpleton—one of the "ain't got nones" of the world with whom I wanted no association. Now, however, I found myself fascinated with her, and fascinated with the gut level of communication which she exhibited. "Billy, are you *gonna* tell me the name of your girlfriend, or am I *gonna* have to beat it out of ya?" "*Gonna*" is a word that I would never use, but it seemed right for her. I had the feeling that she never experienced a loss of words or gave much thought to rightful expression. She didn't care. She knew who she was; she was secure in the knowledge of her job; she loved talking, and she knew how to connect with others.

The experience of chaos in one's life can be a time of crossing barriers. Although I still flinch when I hear terrible grammar, I do not allow it to get in the way of connecting with the person behind the speech. In fact, I find myself tuning in the local country music station to learn and to experience the depth of passion in what can be some of the worst grammar put to song. The feeling *behind* the language, however, is what attracts me now.

"Sue, what has happened to Johnny Dalton? Did he go and get him another wife? I don't know who'd put up with that scoundrel of a man!" In her own way I am sure that she has asked the important questions of life—at least the important ones for her. She may have even found some answers. I don't know. What I do know is that she has a passion for living and a love of her work that shines through the very core of her being. And . . . *we connected.*

"Perhaps the most fundamental law is that we are all related," writes Brenda Schaeffer. "We have no meaning as isolated entities and can only be understood in the context of our relationships" (*Loving Me, Loving You*). I am a part of John, my friend at the local pub; of those poor children on the streets of Belize City; of that man on the grate in front of the Justice Department, and of the waitress at Woolworth's. And they are a part of me. No person is an island unto him or herself. "Each is a piece of the continent, a part of the main," writes John Donne, and "if a clod be washed away by the sea, Europe is the less." And then Donne, who was dean of St. Paul's Cathedral in London when these words were written, expresses what is, perhaps, his most memorable line, and one which Ernest Hemingway made famous: "Never send to ask for whom the bell tolls; it tolls for thee"(*Devotions* by John Donne). In John Donne's England the bells of the church would ring when someone died. He is relating the spiritual truth that we need not ask who has died, for a part of us has died. Each of us experiences death whenever a fellow human being passes from this earthly sphere.

To find oneself outside of oneself is risky business. How we thought of ourselves in the past may become a thing of the past. Old patterns which were once sustaining can break, and we may take risks with our physical being in order to intensify the quest of our spiritual being. "It is only by risking our persons from one hour to another," writes William James, "that we live at all." To live in this sense of "risky vitality" and passion means that fear will become less and less a controlling entity in our lives as we venture into new spiritual territory. We can "learn who we are in the very process of not thinking about who we are," and come to know, experientially, the same truth about *Universal Love* that John Woolman discovered:

> Our gracious Creator cares and provides for all his creatures. His tender mercies are over all his works; and, so far as his love influences our minds, so far we become interested in his workmanship, and feel a desire to take hold of every opportunity to lessen the distresses of the afflicted and increase the happiness of the Creation. Here we have a prospect of one common interest from which our own is inseparable, that *to turn all the treasures we possess into the channel of Universal Love becomes the business of our lives.* (A Plea for the Poor)

• • •

A COVENANT OF DISCIPLINE

There will be no love of the difficult without a frank acceptance of discipline in our lives.
— D. ELTON TRUEBLOOD

ONE OF THE MOST meaningful speeches I ever heard Elton Trueblood deliver was titled, "Learn to Love the Difficult." It was an interesting choice of topic for an audience of five hundred students—young people who were reared in a society in which comfort, pleasure, and freedom from pain and difficulty had become the operating norm.

In his clear and prophetic way, Elton Trueblood challenged the contemporary desire to get by with doing as little as possible and what he called the national preoccupation with searching for a personal comfort zone. He asked these students to consider the possibility of finding spiritual fulfillment in the difficult. His suggestions ranged far: from the study of intellectual and spiritual giants, to the challenge of learning a second or third language, to the practice of a personal discipline of regular prayer, scripture reading, and service. The point he emphasized was that if any growth—spiritual, mental, or physical—is to take place, it will involve discipline.

The love of the difficult is an idea that is tied to one of the most striking paradoxes of the human condition: *Self fulfillment can come through self-denial.* This is an alien concept in a society where the "you can have it all" mentality can be all-consuming. The materialism which surrounds North Americans makes it difficult to live out the injunction of Henry David Thoreau—"Simplify, simplify, simplify." To love the difficult in a complex, gluttonous consumer culture, involves working toward simplification.

In the past few years I have been intrigued with the idea of self-denial through the spiritual discipline of fasting. Perhaps it is because I know what it feels like to deny myself food, having dieted to lose over forty pounds. During this particular time of self-imposed exile from the large portions of sweets and starches that my body was consuming, I was not only losing weight, but I was feeling more spiritually fit as well. Although my first concern was to shed some excess pounds, I did, indeed, feel "cleansed" and closer to God because I was not constantly catering to the pangs of hunger emanating from the physical self.

In twentith-century America the idea of fasting from food in order to grow spiritually seems archaic. The focus on food in our society, perpetuated by the very powerful food industry, has made the concept of fasting seem outdated. If there is to be a revival of interest in recovering the spiritual discipline of fasting from food in order to grow spiritually, it is important to know just how great the forces of opposition are—from the "pitch-in" dinners at our churches, to the Big

Mac's moving across our television screen, tantalizing our taste buds through visual manipulation.

Fasting from food, however, is only *one* love of the difficult spiritual disciplines. *The recovery of passion on the quest for spiritual intimacy involves fasting from anything or any attitude that gets in the way of a closer relationship with God.* I was introduced to the idea of "fasting twentith-century style" by Richard Foster. I am grateful to him for his contemporary message on discipline in the spiritual life, which culminates in his book, *Celebration of Discipline.* But I have been particularly helped by his concern about how the ancient spiritual discipline of fasting needs to be revived and to become enlarged beyond just the idea of fasting from food. "What are the outward things and inner attitudes that separate us from a closer relationship to God, and stifle passion along the spiritual quest?" Each person will have his or her own list, but there are some general areas in our modern culture to which we can all relate.

1. The Media

WE LIVE IN the age of information. We know more about what is happening in the world than we have ever known. Twenty-four-hour television news keeps us informed on every late-breaking story from anywhere in the world. The television anchormen and anchorwomen are the high priests and priestesses of this information cult. They are able to keep our attention by making the *news* an entertainment event that keeps us coming back for more. It is addictive. The more we know, the more we *want* to know. The spiritual question to be asked is, "Is it important for me to know?"

Rufus Jones was the author of spiritual books of an earlier generation, which focused primarily on mysticism. One of the many stories I remember about this man was that he would read his newspaper standing up. The reason being that when he would sit down to read, he wanted to have more substantive reading material that would help him grow spiritually.

Before my mother was diagnosed with severe dementia, she had an annoying habit of keeping the Cable News Network on throughout her waking hours. It was not uncommon to receive telephone calls from her during the day, the sole purpose being to inform me of what was going on in the world. I restrained myself from blurting out, "I don't care!" Just how much information is enough?

2. The Telephone

COUPLED WITH THIS age of information is the age of communication. With the invention of the cellular phone, we can now roam the world and *never*, even in the most remote outback of Australia, or in the dense rain forest of Brazil, be out of touch with whoever wants to reach us.

My mentor had a switch in his study where he could "turn off" the ringing of his phone when he wanted to read, study, write, pray, or just be left alone. He knew what many of us are still learning, that the telephone is both a curse and a blessing which ought to be controlled, and not left alone to be the controller.

3. Loud Music

ONE OF THE MOST singular addictions of our age is rock music. We are bombarded with it. Young people are especially attracted to it, and the louder the better. It screams at us from the compact disc player at home, through the radios of our automobiles, and through television images of "music video." Fasting from loud music and learning to appreciate the beauty of silence, may be one of the most difficult disciplines that this generation attempts.

Outward intruders on our spiritual lives such as the

media, the telephone, and loud music represent one type of barrier that can detract us from the quest for spiritual intimacy. Another type of intruder is *inward*. These intruders are attitudes or behavioral patterns that separate us from God. Once again, each of us will have our own list, but there are some common problems.

1. Criticism

WE LIVE IN a critical time, when we are overly critical of ourselves and others. Of course, there is positive criticism and negative criticism. We can all use positive criticism to improve our work and to help us grow. When it is done out of a sincere, loving concern, it can be helpful. Unfortunately, much negative criticism is expressed under the guise of positive criticism, and can "tear down" rather than "build up." It often seems so natural to attack critically a colleague or family member that it is done before we realize what we have done.

While studying at Princeton, I witnessed a most cruel academic attack on a fellow student. A colleague had prepared for several days, or perhaps weeks, to defend a case-study before his peers and professor. As we waited for the professor to arrive, we were all joking and sharing with one another, getting caught up on our activities from the night before. Finally, the professor arrived, obviously tired, and wanting to be anywhere other than in our class. He carried with him my colleague's printed case-study. As he sat down, he threw the case-study across the table at my friend, asking, "What is this shit?!" We were all stunned, and my colleague was shattered. After class, I invited him to meet me for some coffee.

We met a few blocks from the seminary at the Nassau Inn, and discussed what he had been through. He was still visibly shaken, and toward the close of our conversation, he said, "Jim, I have never been able to learn when I have been put down. I become immobilized." Most of us are the same way. Encouragement, in whatever form, and however slight, is far more helpful to the learning process than negative "academic hazing." The love of the difficult, self-denying path, especially in the world of academia, is to fast from the negative criticism of one another, and focus on how we can be encouraging of one another.

2. Worldly Recognition

THE HUNGER FOR worldly recognition seems in direct contradiction to the quest for spiritual intimacy. Within the Christian world this hunger has been with us for a long time. The first ministers of the gospel, the twelve disciples, were the most common of men. (It is interesting to note that Jesus did not choose one priest to be a member of the chosen twelve, a fact that should be humbling to all who claim the term "religious leader.") And yet, it did not take long for these "commoners" to start arguing about who was the greatest, and then later to professionalize what had been an amateur operation. The Christian movement soon had its own class of religious elite who would clamor for the worldly recognition of their gifts. The holy men were "pedestalized" (my term for being placed ten feet above contradiction) and "reverend," i.e., to be revered crept into our religious language. Why do we care? What is there within us that curries such favor?

There are, of course, many other things and attitudes that get in the way of the recovery of passion and the quest for spiritual intimacy. Loving the difficult and fasting from anything or any attitude which has become entrenched in one's life, is never easy. We know from experience and the spiritual lives of those who have gone before us, however, that the rewards of such a love of the difficult and fasting will move us into a deeper spirituality. By the removal of each barrier to greater spiritual intimacy we are brought into a closer relationship with God, and a better understanding of our spiritual purpose.

As a practical step in helping to recover passion via such a love of the difficult, the following "Covenant of Discipline" may be helpful:

Physical Disciplines

1. I will be careful as to what I eat, recognizing that what I consume directly affects how I feel. I will *not* overeat.
2. I will exercise regularly, at least twenty minutes per day.
3. I will consult with a physician routinely, getting a physical checkup at least once a year.

Mental Disciplines

1. I will read at least one hundred pages per week in the field of religious study and spirituality, and one hundred pages per week in other disciplines.
2. I will join a study group in which I can share my ideas and test my conclusions regarding what I have read.
3. I will attend at least two continuing education events per year to keep me abreast of new developments in my field of employment.

Spiritual Disciplines

1. I will sit in silent, expectant waiting for at least fifteen minutes each day.
2. I will study the great spiritual models of history by reading the classics of religious devotion.
3. I will consciously work at "fasting" from those things, both inward and outward, that inhibit my relationship with God; for example, the television, idle conversation, and negative criticism.
4. I will invite two friends to meet with me weekly in a spiritual support group in which I can openly share my

personal cares and concerns without fear of ridicule or breach of trust.

By learning to love the difficult, by applying discipline to every dimension of our lives, we can learn one of the great truths of the ages: *Nothing of any spiritual importance is easy.*

In the formation of community—finding connection in a disconnected world; in spiritual friendships; by moving beyond our particular cultural context to find ourselves outside of ourselves, and by developing a covenant of discipline—we can begin to recover passion out of our chaos, and it can be tinged with the sacred. In the end, however, only time will bring us to the new life we seek. And so, be patient with yourself and with others. Remain focused on the spiritual, recognizing the transition that you are in is a gift from God. Be respective of the old patterns, for they once served you well. But recovering passion at this point in your life will require new ways. In time, not in your time, but in God's time, a *new* passion will emerge.

Do you remember Johnnie, the man who loved to mow lawns, but can no longer? This isn't exactly true. Johnnie may never be able to mow another lawn and continue to live on this earth, but he could continue to mow, finding meaning and passion in his life once again, until his physical body stops. It is an interesting paradox. To choose *life* may cause *death*. But only the death of the body. The recovery of passion requires a promise to ourselves and to God: *I will not die before I die.*

2

Processing Pain

. . . it is only in that dark night of the soul that you are prepared to see as God sees and love as God loves.

— RAM DASS

A few years ago I heard Mary Cosby, the cofounder of the Church of the Savior in Washington, D.C., speak about the quest for spiritual intimacy. She said that pain needs to be brought to speech, and that where there is no sharing of pain, there can be no intimacy in relationship.

She told the story about a new pastor in the church where her mother was an elder. Just prior to his first Sunday, the pastor went to visit Mary's mother and asked her, "If you could say one thing to me before I enter the pulpit of that great church on Sunday morning, what would it be?" She responded, "Just remember this: Each person that you see, each pair of eyes that you look into as you are speaking, is sitting beside his or her own *pool of tears*."

Each of us sits beside our own *pool of tears*. Some pools are deeper than others, to be sure, but all of us have a pool of our own. Persons who choose to avoid their pain by denial will have difficulty reaching into the hearts of others who are experiencing pain. Pain needs to be brought to speech and shared for intimacy to be experienced, and the tears of transformation need to be shed. By such sharing, chaos is made sacred.

• • •

TEARS OF TRANSFORMATION

Mine eye runneth down with water . . .
— JOHN WOOLMAN

It was Monday night, December 9, 1985. I was startled from a semi-sleep by the ringing telephone. The football game was still on T.V., and I was trying hard to stay awake as the voice of Frank Gifford faded into the background. I reached for the phone on the bed stand, lifted the receiver to my ear, and was told that my father had just been taken to Ball Memorial Hospital in Muncie, Indiana, where he was, at the present moment, undergoing emergency treatment for a serious heart attack.

At the time, my home was in Richmond, forty miles to the southeast of Muncie. Connecting the two cities is U.S. Highway 35. On that particular night in 1985, the highway was shrouded in fog. It was typical weather for Indiana in December—overcast, drizzly, and cold. It was not a pleasant drive, made more difficult by the anxiety I was feeling about my father's condition. Many thoughts were dancing through my mind, and I tried not to think of the worst scenario.

Arriving at the emergency room I was directed by the attendant to a room in the back. Standing outside the room was one of my mother's dearest friends, of whom I asked, "How is he?" In response, she put her head down and motioned me in. My mother was seated next to my brother who had arrived from New Castle minutes before. "Well?" I asked. "He's gone," replied my brother, looking up at me with tears on his cheeks. With this statement of finality I broke down in tears, and for a minute or so the three of us held each other and openly sobbed. The same scene was enacted again when my sister arrived from Indianapolis, and it would be repeated many times with other family members and friends over the next few days.

Dead. My father was dead. Of course I knew the meaning of the word and had been with many families when they had experienced the death of a loved one. This, however, was different. It was my father who had died, and it was my mother who had just lost a husband. Although I knew intellectually that I was entering into one of those transforming moments about which I had spoken and taught, I was not prepared to experience it myself. Ready or not it was happening to me. I was breaking out of my pattern and routine to deal with the tragic unexpected, and God was breaking into my life in a transformational way.

As we walked out of the hospital that evening I noticed that my brother was carrying a large brown grocery bag. "What is that?" I inquired. Stopping under a light, he looked up at me while slowly opening the bag, inviting me to peer in. "It's all that is left," he said. "This and memories." In the bag were my father's familiar black shoes, still shining from the polish he had given them the Saturday night before. His ritual was to always shine shoes on Saturday prior to meeting for worship on Sunday. There was his well-worn billfold and belt. The belt carried the lasting indentation of his expanding midriff. On the top were his carefully folded trousers, and laying across his trousers was his almost new wristwatch. I reached in the bag, removed the watch, and held it in my hand. I was reminded of the opening to the classic cult film of the late sixties, *Easy Rider*, wherein Peter Fonda, sitting atop his motorcycle, threw his watch to the ground in obvious defiance of time, and rode off into the sun. On that night in 1985, feeling nondefiant and grief stricken, I just stood motionless under the brightly lit exit of the hospital emergency room, watching the second hand tick around the circle of the watch. My father's heart had stopped beating at 9:30 P.M., and at 12:01 A.M. his watch was still ticking. It was, for me, an intense moment of transformation. For the first time in my life I was realizing, experientially, that time, unlike the message in the hit song by the Rolling Stones, is not on my side, or my father's side, or any mortal's side. Physical death will, indeed, come to us all sooner or later. And time? It will *continue* . . .

Since I did not cry as a boy, I have had to learn to weep as a man. My father died when I was thirty-six years old. This was the first occasion I can remember when I shed tears as a man. It was the first time that my wife of fifteen years and my daughter who was thirteen years old had ever seen their husband/father cry. It was transformational. With the death of the father, there is the corresponding death of the son, and from this moment on I knew that life would not look the same as it had looked before December 9, 1985.

It has been over twelve years since my father's sudden death. A day does not go by that I don't think of him. I wear his watch as a reminder of my transforming moment outside the emergency room that foggy December night in 1985. It was the beginning of my chaos, and the birth of a pain which continues to this day. The quest for spiritual intimacy runs, necessarily, through the valley of tears.

With the sudden death of my father, I was made cognizant of the pain of our relationship. Sooner or later all children must face the good, bad, and ugly in their relationship with their parents, and it often takes the death of a mother or father to move children into what can be an intense emotional and spiritual experience of sorting out all of the feelings.

On the wall in my office at Plymouth Congregational

Church in Des Moines, hangs a framed picture of a father and son, next to which is a quotation from Moss Hart. It is titled, "Two Lonely People." I keep it above my desk, for it captures the heart of what was my relationship with my father:

> We hurried on, our heads bent against the wind, to the cluster of lights ahead that was 149th Street and Westchester Avenue, and those lights seemed to me the brightest lights I had ever seen. Tugging at my father's coat, I started down the line of pushcarts. . . . I would merely pause before a pushcart to say, with as much control as I could muster, 'Look at that chemistry set!' or, 'There's a stamp album!' or 'Look at the printing press!' Each time my father would pause and ask the pushcart man the price. Then without a word we would move on to the next pushcart. Once or twice he would pick up a toy of some kind and look at it and then at me . . . but I was ten years old and a good deal beyond just a toy; my heart was set on a chemistry set or a printing press. There they were on every pushcart we stopped at, but the price was always the same . . . soon I looked up and saw we were nearing the end of the line. Only two or three more pushcarts remained. My father looked up, too, and I heard him jingle some coins in his pocket. In a flash I knew it all. He'd gotten together about seventy-five cents to buy me a Christmas present, and he hadn't dared say so in case there was nothing to be had for so small a sum. As I looked up at him I saw a look of despair and disappointment in his eyes that brought me closer to him than I had ever been in my life. I wanted to throw my arms around him and say, 'It doesn't matter . . . I understand. . . . This is better than a chemistry set or a printing press . . . I love you.' But instead we stood shivering beside each other for a moment—then turned away from the last two pushcarts and started silently back home. . . . I didn't even take his hand on the way home nor did he take

mine. We were not on that basis. Nor did I ever tell him how close to him I felt that night—that for a little while the concrete wall between father and son had crumbled away and I knew that we were two lonely people struggling to reach each other. (*Act One*)

Two lonely people struggling to reach each other. In such a father/son relationship I know that I am not alone. It is *painful* to accept and to try and understand. It is in the recognition of such pain, however, that we can begin to become liberated from the shackles of denial, freeing us to continue the quest for spiritual intimacy. I have learned, experientially, the truth of C. G. Jung's words, "There is no coming to consciousness without pain."

The two mistakes we can make with pain are, (1) we spend all of our spiritual and emotional energy trying to get out of it, *or* (2) we perpetuate it because we define our personhood through the eyes of martyrdom. We can avoid spiritual intimacy by taking either of these paths. The processing of pain in a healthy way begins when we become sensitive to when it is time to stay on the cross in order to plumb the depths of our spirits, *and* when it is time to climb down from that cross, prepared to continue the quest.

My tears of transformation began to flow when my father died, and they have continued through any number of other losses experienced since then. The spiritual truth that God touches us in our vulnerability has been made real to me, and it is when we are in pain that we are most vulnerable.

Within the history of the Christian tradition, this truth has many examples. One of the most familiar comes from the experience of Saint Augustine. In his *Confessions* he tells about his transformation through tears. "So was I speaking and weeping in the most bitter contrition of my heart," he writes, "when, lo! I heard from a neighboring house a voice, as of boy or girl, I know not, chanting and oft repeating. 'Take up and read; take up and read.' Instantly, my countenance altered." Augustine interpreted this as a message from God, urging him to pick up his Bible and read. He continues:

> I seized, opened, and in silence read that section on which my eyes first fell. "Not in rioting and drunkenness, not in clambering and wantonness, not in strife and envying; but put ye on the Lord Jesus Christ. . . ." No further would I read; nor needed I: for instantly at the end of this sentence, by a light as it were of serenity infused into my heart, all the darkness of doubt vanished away.

The spiritual quest of St. Augustine became empowered through the tears of transformation.

The author of *A Testament of Devotion*, Thomas Kelly, experienced the tears of transformation following his failure at Harvard University. Kelly was scheduled to defend his doctoral dissertation before a faculty committee. During his academic interrogation, he had what his son referred to in his biography about his father as a "woozy spell." Today we would probably diagnose Kelly's condition as some form of epilepsy. The end result was that he could not answer any of the questions asked of him, and he failed. And not only had he failed, but he was told that he could never again return to Harvard.

Those were difficult words for someone who had given his life to the pursuit of God through reason and philosophy. He left Harvard depressed, so much so that his wife thought that he may take his own life. This was the fall of 1937.

In January of 1938, Thomas Kelly was scheduled to deliver a series of lectures at Germantown Friends Meeting near Philadelphia. As he spoke, his words were surrounded by the authority of one who had experienced, in a transformational way, the living God. This is how he began his first lecture:

To you in this room who are seekers, to you, young and old who have toiled all night and caught nothing, but who want to launch out into the deeps and let down your nets for a draught, I want to speak as simply, as tenderly, as clearly as I can. For God can be found. There is a last rock for your souls, a resting place of absolute peace and joy and power and radiance and security. There is a Divine Center into which your life can slip, a new and absolute orientation in God, a Center where you live with Him and out of which you see all of life, through new and radiant vision, tinged with new sorrows and pangs, new joys unspeakable and full of glory. (A *Testament of Devotion*)

Thomas Kelly moved from mere *knowledge about* the God of history, to *acquaintance with* the God of the immediate present. His tears of transformation began to flow after he had failed academically. His failure had made him vulnerable to a change which was wrought within the very foundation of his soul. And from this time until his premature death three years later, he never ceased living out of his new found spiritual intimacy.

Whether it is experienced in the drama of repentance as illustrated in the life of Augustine, or in the academic failure of Thomas Kelly, pain is processed through the tears of transformation. The tears will flow in moments of unexpected vulnerability, when we are separated from the familiar and are forced to look at life from new perspectives. They can also occur at more expected and natural times in the cycle of life. Whenever they occur, they are cleansing and filled with the fertilizer which makes for new growth. In retrospect, they can be humorous, as well as painful . . .

A few years ago, my wife and I took our only child to college. Alicia's departure from the nest left a very quiet home. Her college of choice was called Hope, located in Holland, Michigan, five-and-a-half hours north of Richmond, Indiana, where we were living.

When we arrived at her dormitory we were greeted by a campus policeman and three or four sophomores assigned to the "orientation team." The sophomores helped us unload the van, which contained my daughter's remote control television, small refrigerator, stereo set and speakers, "Jam Box", a rug, all kinds of clothes, snack food and pop, and four boxes of personal computer paraphernalia. Do you remember when we went to college with a suitcase and portable Smith–Corona? The times have changed.

We helped Alicia unpack, but anxious for her to get acquainted with her two roommates, we left so they could be alone. We were not comforted by the fact that we noticed one of her roommates was reading something called *Vampire Notes*, and enjoyed listening to rock groups called Megadeath and Slayer! We made arrangements to meet Alicia at her dorm the next morning so that we could take her to breakfast.

In the morning we arrived a few minutes early but Alicia was already waiting. As a parent in this situation, there are certain things that you hope you will not hear the first thing after the first day of your daughter's first year in college. One of them is, "I hate my roommates." We were not so lucky. As she climbed into the car, Alicia said, and this is a direct quotation, "I can't stand them! I hate them! I hate them! I hate them!" With visions of $1000 checks to Hope College flying off into the clouds, my wife and I tried to calm her. "We know you are upset now, but give it a little time!" And, "You are tired now. I am sure that things will get better."

All during breakfast we listened to horror stories. ("Did you know this college has a "rape van" to carry students at night?") She openly talked of going back to Indiana with us. We finally calmed her sufficiently to be able to take her to the next orientation session. We blew kisses to her as we shoved her out of the car, prying each of her fingers off the door, and then speeding away quickly, yelling, "We'll be back in an hour. You are going to be fine!"

It got better. It got worse. It got better again. It was a roller coaster weekend of mixed emotions. Before we left on Sunday morning, there was a slight uplift in her spirits. She said that she was going to invite her roommates to dinner, and she was looking forward to a freshman party. We hugged, kept a stiff upper lip, and said goodbye. We drove away, and she turned and went back into her dormitory. Then ... we cried. It was a *tear-fest* from Holland, Michigan, to Richmond. Do you remember when Alicia did this? ... Do you remember when Alicia did that? ... Do you remember what she was like at age five?—all the way home. We were experiencing the tears of transformation.

Coming and going—arriving and departing—are a part of the rhythm of life. We start school and we graduate. We begin a vocation and we retire. We rear children and they leave home for college. We are born and we die. At each point of transition the tears will come, for patterns will be broken, and life will change. Processing the pain of such transition through the tears of transformation, helps to make the chaos experienced sacred.

• • •

THE WOMB OF FEAR

And the angel said to them, "Be not afraid ..."
—LUKE 2:10

We are afraid not to fear. Whenever God breaks through and becomes incarnate in our lives, *fear* will be a natural response. Why? Because humans are patterned creatures, and God is a pattern breaker. In my experience, the quest for spiritual intimacy has been stifled when I have succumbed to my fears, retreating to the womb of fear where I was comfortable. I was also *not* growing. What I now realize is that this comfortable womb of fear will eventually become a *tomb of tears*. When I have faced my fears and *walked through* them, I have continued to grow.

When in chaos, fear and love become clear choices. When faced with loss in our lives and the chaos which it produces, we can choose to close ourselves off from the change and transition around us, curl up in the prenatal position, and weather the storm through denial. Or, we can put our hand into the hand of the loving, incarnate God, *fear not*, and make our chaos sacred. As we process pain, we process our fear as well. We are helped when we realize that the two words used most often together in Scripture are "fear not."

The patterns of our lives are often made as a result of the fears that become boundaries. Some patterns bordered by fear are helpful, such as the fear which keeps us from falling off a cliff. In relationship, however, the borders of fear can be devastating. As we recognized the unhealthy codependency of our relationship, my wife, Elizabeth, and I chose to move beyond our fear boundaries and risk losing one another, rather than to continue in a togetherness which de-energized us both. We were both willing to live into the truth of Brenda Schaeffer's words, "Openness to change can be risky—it can even lead to breakups—but without it, a relationship will lose its vibrancy" (*Is It Love or Is It Addiction*). To take risks in relationship involves facing our fears, especially the fear of *aloneness*.

When the final decision was made to separate, I was in North Carolina. Still trying to medicate my pain through denial, I felt that a change in geography and role would be helpful. I took a sabbatical from Earlham College, and accepted the position of "interim" superintendent of North Carolina Yearly Meeting (Conference) of Friends. It was as "institutional" and "political" a position as one could find. The issues of

"New Age" religion creeping into the Yearly Meeting, as well as lively debates about homosexuality were making for division. I was, to say the least, uninterested in such debates, and therefore began to withdrawal almost immediately upon arrival in Greensboro.

I called my wife two months into my tenure in North Carolina. Although we had had numerous conversations since I had left, this one was different. Both of us were tired of feeling "stuck." There was so much miscommunication and loss of intimacy that we were emotionally wiped out. Swallowing hard, and trembling, I broached the subject. "Elizabeth, if our relationship is to have any hope—either as friends or husband and wife—we need to 'clean the slate,' get a divorce, and see where we end up on the other side." With an expression of exasperation, she agreed. It was over. All had been said.

The emptiness and fear which I felt when I hung up the telephone is difficult to describe. I felt alone. I felt unloved. I felt abandoned in a world which did not feel safe. At the moment, all that I wanted to do was pick up the phone, call my wife back, and tell her how much I loved her and how I wanted to get back together. I didn't. Instead, I turned the radio on and listened to soft music. And . . . *I cried.*

The next morning, following a sleepless night, the telephone rang. It was Elizabeth. She was crying uncontrollably, and repeated between sobs, "I just can't take it anymore. I want to die." My wife had had bouts of depression before, but this was different. It was as bad as I had ever heard her. My natural instinct was to "rescue" her, assure her that I will not leave her and that I would return home. Instead, I felt a presence of light and strength, and said to her, "Elizabeth, fear not . . . fear not . . . fear not." I was brought to tears by her weeping. We cried together, while I kept repeating, "fear not." I concluded our conversation by asking her to call her workplace and tell her supervisor that she was not coming in, and then asked her to go back to bed. She said that she would. I told her that I loved her, and then hung up. I quickly dressed into my running shorts, and left my apartment for the park to run.

All day long I prayed for Elizabeth. I was in terrible emotional pain, but I knew that we could not go back to the fearful patterns of the past, wherein we rescued one another, without openness and honesty, or without taking responsibility and working through the pain as our own. There is a line in the traditional wedding ceremony which reads, "You will from henceforth live a blended life, which will divide your sorrows and multiply your satisfactions." Throughout our married life the sorrows were not faced honestly, nor divided mutually, and the satisfactions had lost their ability to arouse passion. We both realized that we could not go back to the deadness of the past.

In the early evening Elizabeth called. "Jim, I want to thank you for your words this morning," she began. "They saved my life." I thanked her for her openness and honesty in the way she shared her feelings, and also for the love and support I had felt from her. We did not, for the first time in our married life together, retreat to the *womb of fear*. One definition of insanity is to repeat patterns over and over again, even though the intended outcome never materializes. Fear keeps us trapped in such patterns. To experience the best in relationship and in all of life, we must risk the breaking of patterns, even though we do not know what is beyond them. As painful as *honesty* can be, and however acute the pain feels when we are honest about our feelings, it is ever so much better than the dishonest, chronic pain of denial. As a result of my experience, I am convinced that the path to intimacy in relationship, whether that intimacy is physical or spiritual, passes through the gate of openness and honesty. And it is risky. To live, however, to *truly live* is to risk from moment to moment. If we are not willing to risk, we are not willing to live. I knew this truth in my professional life. I was now experiencing it in my personal life.

It has been one year since our formal separation and eventual divorce. Both of us have grown considerably in the past twelve months, recognizing that our love for one another is very different from the fearful codependency we once believed was love. We have been growing spiritually in ways we didn't know were possible. It has been a time of aloneness, to be sure, and the loneliness can, at times, be devastating. Now, however, when we seek what we need from one another, it is without all of the negative baggage of the past, which, upon reflection, was so detrimental to our relationship. Openness about our feelings and truthfulness about our individual needs has moved each of us into an intimacy that has never before been experienced. Relationship, we have learned, is a dance between autonomy and togetherness, each recognizing the individuation of the other, and the formation of a *new* person when we are together—a newness which does not take away from each of our beings, but makes someone entirely *new*.

The play *Harvey* by Mary Chase is about Elwood P. Dowd, an eccentric man, who drank quite a bit. His closest friend is an enormous white rabbit called Harvey—who is unseen for the most part by anyone but Elwood. Elwood's family hired Dr. Chumley, a psychiatrist, to cure Elwood and rid the family of Harvey's embarrassing presence. But being a good psychiatrist, and therefore willing to move beyond the boundaries which fear the unknown, Dr. Chumley had a spectacular conversion. Finally, in one scene, he blurts out and says, "Flyspecks. I've been spending my life among flyspecks while *miracles* [Harvey] have been leaning on lamp posts" (*Harvey: Comedy in Three Acts*).

The miracles of life are discovered beyond the boundaries of fear which we have set in our lives. Breaking patterns, with

God's help—fear not—is to move beyond the flyspecks in which we have been existing. "Sooner or later," writes Jack Kornfield, "we have to learn to let go and allow the changing mystery of life to move through us without our fearing it, without holding or grasping"(A Path with Heart). Chaos is the environment for pattern breaking, where we can "allow the changing mystery of life to move through us . . ." It may not mean the radical relational work through which my chaos moved me, but whatever boundary of fear we break, we will find ourselves hanging around lamp posts a lot more, ready to experience the miracles which will most certainly occur.

• • •

HEALING THE SCARS OF THE SOUL

Healing is not a simple or an overnight process.
It is a life's work, as we grow in our ability to allow
love into our injured hearts.
— RUTH SCHWEITZER-MORDECAI

It was the late John Chancellor of NBC News who said, "If you want to make God laugh, tell Him your plans." This statement was made at the time of his retirement, when he had just learned that he had terminal cancer. Life is filled with such tragedy, when the plans that we have made get thwarted because of an unexpected turn of events. Persons with whom we have planned and with whom we have worked side by side, die too soon. Relationships that once seemed solid, fall apart. Promises that we felt were sure and impregnable, are not kept. Hope can quickly become hopelessness. If we live long enough, we will know such experiences.

The future is never sure, and the present is always changing. The only things on which we can count have already occurred.

My life was once a straight path, today passing into tomorrow, sure, secure, and predictable. The straight path I was on was one of problem-fixer and caretaker. The more I was needed to fix things and make them all right again, the more my life felt justified. Nothing seemed to be beyond my capability. The course of my life could have been compared to the person who performs in the circus by spinning plates on sticks. Just as I finished adding a new plate, the first stick needed another twist to keep it spinning. Whether it was my marriage, fatherhood, managing the Yokefellow Movement (a church and individual renewal organization founded by D. Elton Trueblood), teaching at the Earlham School of Religion, speaking and leading seminars around the country, or keeping my mentor pleased with my work, there seemed to be no end to the number of plates which I could add to my life. My wife would meet me at the door of our home with an airline ticket and a clean bag of clothes, while she took a bag of dirty clothes and a used airline ticket from my hands. The way in which I could keep everything spinning amazed even the most skeptical. Workaholism medicated my pain, and I received added strength when someone would affirm me by saying, "Jim, I don't know how you do it all!" I didn't either. It wasn't what I had written, but *how many* books I had published. It wasn't so much what I had learned, but *how many* degrees hung on my wall. Life was achievement which could be measured outwardly by the number of awards I had received, and the *Who's Who* books in which I was included. All was well in my little world.

And then my father died of a massive heart attack at the age of sixty-two. My teacher and mentor, with whom I had worked closely for ten years, moved to a retirement home in Pennsylvania. My wife went into depression; my mother was diagnosed with severe dementia, and my daughter, who had left for college in Michigan one and a half years before, filled with hope and excitement, was now back home with no sense of direction. My life was becoming chaotic. As I was struggling ever more diligently to keep the plates spinning, my mentor died and I went through a divorce, thus completing my litany of loss, and sending me to the floor with plates crashing down all around.

Reflecting on the new realities which life forced upon me, and the chaos into which I was thrown, I know that it is not *automatic* that any one of us survive, spiritually or mentally, from such loss. But there are ways to make small beginnings to heal the scars that such turmoil can cause our souls.

At first I avoided my pain. I went into denial, even denying that I needed to talk to anyone about my losses. After all, people would come to *me* for help and counsel. Surely, I thought, I didn't need help. And yet, of course, I did. As a colleague of mine has said, "Denial is not a river in Egypt." There are experiences in our lives when the mechanism of denial can be of help . . . for a while. God has given each of us an amazing array of ways to cope with what life deals us, and in some circumstances denial can be used in helpful ways when the pain is overbearing. But if it becomes a permanent state, the suppression of the pain will overwhelm us, and it will eventually destroy our ability to function. On the whole, the deeper and faster we face and move into our pain, the sooner we can begin the process of healing. As Thomas Merton has written, "The truth that many people never understand until it is too late is that the more you try to avoid suffering the more you suffer" (*Love and Living*). I went to see a spiritual counselor who helped me face my pain and denial, beginning with the death of my father.

Before I experienced it myself, I had no idea of the importance of viewing my father—dead—lying in the coffin. I remember a nurse in the emergency room at the hospital asking me if I wanted to see my father after he had been pronounced dead. I declined. I did, however, live in a state of some denial for the next two days, half expecting him to walk through the door as I had seen him do so many times before. I remember thinking, "He's just lost. He will be back." And then I went to the mortuary and faced his earthly demise head-on, and at the same time was able to bring his physical existence in my life to closure. The pain was acute, but the healing process had begun.

The longer I live, the more important *forgiveness* becomes to my spiritual and emotional health. As we accept our pain, being open and honest about what we are feeling and experiencing, we will learn that forgiveness can be a primary factor in making the pain bearable. Forgiveness is not just a medication for our pain, but a *process* which can lead to healing our souls.

If blame is sought, and the hurts and ills that are bound to come in life are calculated, building up within our injured hearts, we will eventually damage our souls. Jesus knew this, making forgiveness a basic tenet in his teaching. Responding to a question from Peter, "Lord, how often shall my brother sin against me, and I forgive him? As many as seven times?" Jesus said, "I do not say to you seven times, but *seventy times seven*" (Matt. 18:21–22). In other words, forgiveness has no end. No one can forgive four hundred ninety times without it becoming an integral part of his or her very being.

As Elizabeth and I moved toward separation, we vowed not to fall into the familiar pattern of many of our friends who were going through the same thing, using anger and vile language against one another. We loved each other too much for that to happen. As we traveled through the various stages of such a life-experience calamity, which is very painful regardless of the situation, *forgiveness* became central to our spiritual and mental health. Friends would become more supportive of me or her, but when hostile words were spoken against one or the other of us, we would not join in.

Coupled with the forgiveness of one another, for whatever ills or pain each inflicted upon the other, was an attitude of *repentance*. There are at least two things in life that cannot be overdone—expressions of gratitude and expressions of repentance. All of us have harmed others over the years, intentionally or unintentionally, and so saying "I am sorry" cannot be said too often. It frees the soul from the darkness of blame and the defensiveness of the hurt we feel. It is all right to express justified anger, but when such anger is wrapped in vengeance and a defensive transference of responsibility for "our lot in life," then it will harm our souls. As Melody Beattie has written, "Real power comes when we stop holding others responsible for our pain, and we take responsibility for all our feelings" (*The Language of Letting Go*).

The story of the prodigal son (Luke 15:11–32) goes to the heart of the healing of pain. It was nothing less than courageous for the father in the story to accept his wandering son back home, even after he had squandered his inheritance and denied his responsibility in the family system. How much more natural it would have been for the father to have made him pay for his indiscretions, rather than celebrate his return home with a party. In this story, more so than in any other, a *new ethic* of love, repentance, and forgiveness is modeled for us. It is a story for the soul, and helps us recognize that there are no more meaningful words in our language than, *"I am sorry. You are forgiven."*

As in the recovery of passion, our pain is processed and the scars on the soul are healed by way of spiritual friendship. We don't have to manage our stories by ourselves. We can share our stories of pain, and experience the care and love of those who can relate to what we are going through.

Patrick Henry, Jr., director of the Ecumenical Institute in

Collegeville, Minnesota, recently delivered the Baccalaureate Address at Southern Methodist University. He shared from the autobiography of Gilda Radner, of "Saturday Night Live" fame, who died a few years ago of ovarian cancer. His address was titled, "Delicious Ambiguity," and he began by quoting these words from Radner:

> I wanted to be able to write on the book cover: "Her triumph over cancer," or "She wins the cancer war." I wanted a perfect ending. Now I've learned the hard way, that some poems don't rhyme and some stories don't have a clear beginning, middle and end. Like my life, this book is about not knowing, having to change, taking the moment and making the best of it, without knowing what's going to happen next. "Delicious ambiguity," as Joanna said. (*It's Always Something*)

The Joanna referred to is Joanna Bull, assistant director of the Wellness Community. The community became a place of support and healing for Radner as she went through the pain of her physical decline. Joanna Bull kept reminding her, "I just want you to know that you are not alone." *You are not alone. We are not alone.* The scars of the soul can be healed in community and in spiritual friendship where the painful ambiguities which life thrusts upon us can become "delicious."

There is a wonderful story about the great scientist and academic, Albert Einstein, who was on a train out of New York City. As the conductor came through the passenger coaches, Dr. Einstein began to look frantically through his coat pockets for his ticket. By the time that the conductor arrived at where Einstein was seated, the renowned scientist had pulled out all of his pockets in both his trousers and coat, and was proceeding to search through his briefcase. The conductor, immediately recognizing who Einstein was, said, "Don't worry Dr. Einstein, I trust you," and proceeded to collect the tickets of the rest of the passengers. After about thirty minutes, the conductor, having finished his ticket collection, was walking back through the car where Einstein was located. By this time the Princeton professor was blocking the aisle, down on his hands and knees, looking and feeling under seats and baggage for his ticket. The conductor reiterated, "Dr. Einstein, please don't worry about finding your ticket. I told you that I trust you." To this, Einstein turned his head upward from his position on the floor and said, "Young man, this is not an issue of trust. It is an issue of direction. I have no idea where I am going!"

When we become clear about the issue of direction, turning our attention to the present and future, the healing process is stimulated. After we grieve the pain of the past—for a while—our healing is enhanced when we close the doors behind us. If the soul is not evoked into the present and future, we can become stuck, thus missing the spiritual opportunities and lessons to be learned from our pain. We can also become insensitive to the movement of God into the future.

An elderly friend was moving to another state. The home he was leaving was one in which he had lived for over forty years. It would be a difficult move for anyone, but for a man in his eighties, it was nearly devastating. Caught in the middle of this parting, he said to me, "I am cleaning out my desk and packing my books. It is killing me." And yet, following his lament, he was able to evoke his soul into the future, recognizing that God was opening new doors of growth for him. He knew the direction in which he needed to go. The natural response for many would have been to stay stuck in the past, focusing on the pain that such a dramatic move was causing. But my friend believed in a God of process—of movement and journey—and he knew that life is ambiguous. The choice was to live in the past, fearfully holding on to the familiar, or to evoke the soul into the future of possibility where healing can take place and where new adventures are yet to be born. To his benefit, my friend chose the later.

And, finally, a word about *patience*. "Patient endurance attaineth to all things," wrote Sister Teresa. This may be an overstatement, but the importance of patience in healing cannot be ignored. It is impossible to *force* the scars on our souls into healing by the limitations of earthly time. To evoke the soul out of the painful past and into the present and future possibility of healing is not something that is done hurriedly or all at once. Healing the scars on the soul is not like taking a pill for a headache. *Soul-aches* are something very different and require patience, recognizing that "the wheels of God grind slowly, but they grind exceedingly fine." It is here that those of us in Western culture have difficulty. "Slow" is a rare word in our vocabulary.

Jean Adriel has written about leaving her spiritual teacher, Meher Baba:

> The parting from Baba was an extremely painful one. In my farewell moments with him I was moved to thank him for all the joy and pain of my life with him, to which he replied: "Thank me only for the pain." Now, years later, I fully appreciate the wisdom of these words. The expression 'growing pain' is just as applicable to the spiritual life as it is to the physical, and without it no growth is possible for the human creature.

Life is an accumulation of scars. Healing our scars is a continuous process of growing "in our ability to allow love into our injured hearts" (Ruth Schweitzer-Mordecai, *Spiritual Freedom*). *Love.* . . . It is what makes working through our pain possible. We will never be free of pain, for it is a basic ingredient of life. Each pain experienced carries a special place in our hearts, not to be forgotten. It is one of the essential ways we learn and grow on our quest for spiritual intimacy. When we *process* our pain, bringing it to speech, sharing it, and not denying what we are experiencing, we can move from being immobilized by it, to being emboldened, evoking us into new life and growth. Pain will come, but it will never entirely go. It makes for an ever deepening experience of spiritual growth, and something (perhaps years later, as with Jean Adriel), for which we can be grateful.

And so, do not deny your pain; forgive, repent, and love; express your pain to spiritual friends and recognize that you are not alone; close the door on the painful past, evoking the soul into the present and future where healing can take place. And be patient. We need not become frantic as the ambiguities of life are thrust upon us. Remember, God loves us and suffers with us, and within the midst of the calamity occurring in our lives, we "are encircled by the arms of the mystery of God" (Hildegarde of Bingen).

3

Exploring Prayer

*If we love God, if we acknowledge to whom we belong, if in the
intervals of other tasks this love moves steadily to the surface,
and gives a glow to all we do, this is prayer without ceasing.*
— DOUGLAS V. STEERE

We are living in a time of transition and change, when everything is open to question, even the most basic spiritual pillars undergirding Western civilization. Old denominational allegiances no longer stir any strong loyalties; there is an aggressiveness on the part of radicals on the edge of liberation theology, and a defensive militancy on the part of old order conservatives. In brief, the well-defined patterns of life which have sustained generations, no longer hold the meaning that they once did.

All across the religious landscape, new spiritual possibilities are being sought. As a result of the chaos being felt, millions of pilgrims have set out on an inward spiritual quest, which, they hope, will help to define their lives outwardly. "Out in front of us," wrote Thomas Kelly,

> is the drama of people and of nations, seething, struggling, laboring, dying. Upon this tragic drama . . . our eyes are all set in anxious watchfulness and in prayer. But within the

silences of the souls of persons an eternal drama is ever being enacted, in these days as well as in others. And on the outcome of this inner drama rests, ultimately, the outer pageant of history. (*A Testament of Devotion*)

The "inner drama" of which Thomas Kelly has so beautifully written is forever unfolding. In many ways he echoes the words of St. Augustine, who wrote following the destruction of Rome: "All earthly cities are vulnerable. People build them and people destroy them. At the same there is the city of God which people did not build and cannot destroy, and which is everlasting" (*The City of God*).

The new spiritual inner quest which is emerging out of the chaos, invariably moves us into an exploration of prayer. The common understanding of prayer is narrow in scope and short on expectation. The style of prayer which begins, "Now I lay me down to sleep . . . ," or issues in countless requests, from a good grade on an exam to the healing of cancer, is *not* what exploring prayer means here. My attempt in this chapter is to broaden the meaning of the term *prayer*, incorporating the process of seeking, and the miracle of spiritual transformation. Prayer, as I define it, is the vehicle used in the search for a finite/Infinite connection. And such a search has many dimensions.

· · ·

SILENCE, WAITING, AND EXPECTANCY

Be still and know that I am God.
— PSALM 46:10

There is a sign in front of the Friends Meetinghouse in Cambridge, England which reads, "Don't just do something . . . SIT!" In an age when "busyness" is equated with productivity, and workaholics and playaholics are the two areas of addiction toward which people in our culture gravitate, it seems important advice. And, I must admit, that I am one who has great difficulty sitting and waiting for anything. The immortal words of William Penn hound me—"Time is what we want most, but what, alas, we use worst, and for which God will surely most strictly reckon with us when time shall be no more"(*Fruits of Solitude*). I think that Penn was a workaholic.

I love to . . .

—arrive at a theater just as the movie begins.

—step into an elevator just as the door is closing.

—arrive in a bank or grocery store just as the clerk opens a new line.

—enter a meeting just as it is called to order.

—meet a publishing deadline with a minute to spare.

—be the first in line at a traffic light, so that when it turns green I don't have to wait on the cars in front of me to go.

Following each of these experiences, I can't help but feel a slight smile of smugness come over my face, for I have beaten the system and the odds which are stacked against me. The norm in life is waiting: waiting for the bus . . . waiting for the elevator . . . waiting in the bank drive-up lane.

A couple of summers ago I was in London, and I needed a taxi. I found the line, or queue, and began the tedious process of waiting my turn. The polite way in which the English will form a queue and wait their rightful turn is an amazing thing to observe. Ahead of me was a gentleman who was calmly reading a book, completely oblivious to the hustle and bustle of the world around him. He was content to wait, absorbed in his book. And me? I was fidgeting the whole time, getting more irritated the longer I stood there. The gentleman with the book knew the art of patience and waiting within the system. I did not.

I learned a most important lesson that day in the taxi queue. As I stood there observing the man with the book, I vowed never again to stand next to someone so patient. I will, instead, look for another disgruntled, impatient person with whom I can gripe—preferably a North American. It makes the time of waiting go ever so much faster.

Don't just do something . . . sit! Although I am still working on the discipline of sitting and waiting in expectant silence, I recognize it as an important step in the exploration of prayer. Since no spiritual discipline is ever fully grasped, but always "in process" of developing within us, I will proceed. I enter this realm with some fear and trembling, but with the knowledge that it is a discipline which can help to make our chaos sacred, and empower our quest for spiritual intimacy. I believe that it has a lot to do with questions that are bothering many people today, such as, "Why is God not more real to me?" Or, "Why do I have difficulty feeling God's presence in my life?" and "Why do I feel that God has abandoned me in my chaos?"

By and large, Western civilization is one of activism. The fast pace of life and sense of urgency affects us all—in our homes, our work, our politics, and our places of worship and service. There have been times in my life when the busiest place I visit all week is a Sunday morning worship service! Activism and dynamism, which is obsessed with speed and change, can dull our senses and our response to the "still small voice" of the living God. I remember seeing a cartoon in *The New Yorker* some years ago, which showed a North American couple rushing up the steps of the Louvre in Paris, shouting, "Quick, show us the Mona Lisa, we're double-parked!" As with most cartoons, this is funny because it smacks of reality.

At the core of the new spirituality being sought is the desire to be connected with the Infinite, i.e., to know and to be known by the living God. There is a tremendous hunger today for an experience with a God who is personal, not remote; who moves us emotionally, not merely intellectually, and whose Spirit can be a constant source of strength in a material world which is spiritually depleting. The plea to "make God personal" is one that is being made in ever greater frequency.

Marcus J. Borg tells about being asked to speak before an Episcopal men's group: "Because of the nature of the group, whose times together were marked by personal sharing, their instructions were twofold: 'Talk to us about Jesus, and *make it personal* '" (*Meeting Jesus Again for the First Time*). The history of religion is filled with reformation and renewal experiences which begin with a movement back to the basics of a personal and direct experience with the living God. Overemphasis upon ritual, debate over peripheral issues of belief, and the cumbersome work of institutional religion have all contributed to the inner quest for a personal, spiritual intimacy.

My father would often tell the story about the tourists from Midwestern America who were being guided through Westminster Abbey in London. The guide had spoken for about an hour concerning the architecture and the beauty of the windows, as well as telling about all of the historical figures who are buried there. Finally, a woman in the group interrupted the guide saying, "This is all very well, young man, but has anyone been *saved* here lately?" Although the language seems archaic, this woman knew how to move from a focus on mere tradition to a focus on what is spiritually significant. For millions of pilgrims today who are experiencing a sense of chaos in their lives, spiritual significance is centered in a personal relationship with the living God.

Silent, expectant waiting can be one of the best preparations for personal communion with God. The silence itself, of course, has no magic. When coupled with the discipline of *expectant waiting*, however, it can be a time of actual, reciprocal correspondence with God. And there are ways to prepare for such expectant waiting.

One such way of preparation can be called *receptivity*. We become receptive to hearing God's "still small voice" when we endeavor to erase *self*, its cares and problems from our hearts and minds. The Hindu becomes receptive through the practice of the eight steps of yoga—sitting firmly without motion on a spot that is neither too high or too low—forbearance, observance, restraint of the senses, steadying of the mind, contemplation, and profound meditation. Each religious tradition will have its own way of becoming receptive, as will each individual. What seems to be important is that the artifacts of *self*— anger, pettiness, selfishness, ambition—be purged from our souls, and replaced by a humble and sincere desire to know and to be known by the living God.

One of the chief reasons *why* so many of our experiences of meditation, prayer, and worship are of little benefit is that we do not *expect* to receive from them, much less to give anything to them. The result can be lethargy, a duty to endure as we slouch with hands in pockets into the presence of the Infinite.

A second manner of preparation has to do with our relationships, i.e., *human love*. When we harbor negative feelings about someone in our life; when we are lacking in love toward our fellow human beings, the windows of the soul can close. This is especially true if the person or persons toward whom one feels anger, suspicion, or just plain old unfriendliness is in the same room. There can be no worse preparation for silent, expectant waiting than nursing a grudge. It has been a helpful practice for me to begin my waiting upon God by thinking of persons in my life whom I dearly love, both those who have died and those who are still living. I have been amazed at how such a practice of loving will flow out of me, as in concentric circles, soon enveloping even those whom I have had difficulty in relating.

There is a third kind of preparation for silent, expectant waiting which is deliberately undertaken, and that is *reading the Bible or other devotional literature.* In using the Bible it is important to be reminded that some sections are much more likely to help than others. The Psalms, the Gospels, and some of the beautiful passages in the Epistles on love, will speak more to our seeking condition than the prophetic and historical sections. Also, because poets are usually filled with mystery and spiritual wonder, poetry can be a wonderful resource of preparation.

Finally, we are helped by our *dreams.* At times they are difficult to remember, but when we do, they can be instructive spiritual guides. As I have experienced chaos, my dreams have become more vivid.

I recently had the most striking and colorful dream I can remember. I was seated in a large convention hall surrounded by around five hundred other persons. The conference was on "Healing," and my father was scheduled to give one of the major addresses. As I sat and waited for the program to begin, a beautiful woman in a long, flowing white dress entered the room. If you can remember the way Loretta Young would enter the set of her television program, then you can envision this woman in my dream. The next thing I knew, we were all standing, and she was touching the foreheads of person after person in row after row. I immediately sensed that she represented the Holy Spirit. Eventually she came to me, touched my forehead, and then proceeded to the open window to my left, and threw into the wind an armload of colorful confetti. The confetti swirled around against the background of a beautiful blue sky, and then formed into a kite. As I stood at the window and watched, the wind took the kite higher and higher. There was no controlling string attached, just the wind blowing the kite beyond view. As the kite disappeared, I awakened.

What the psychiatrist C. G. Jung would think of this, I do not know. I don't really know what to make of it myself. *I only know that it seems important to my own spiritual quest, and I have not been able to forget it* .

Believing that it is an important discipline in preparation for silent, expectant waiting, I have been working hard to pay more attention to what is happening around me in my subconscious world of dreams. My daily prayer has been for God to help me "pay attention" to the ways in which the spiritual is interacting with my physical and emotional world. Silent, expectant waiting has not been an easy discipline for me to learn, and I am not alone. To reflect and savor, linger and lull in the sacrament of the present moment, rather than *sacrificing* the present moment, takes a lot of work for some of us who have been reared with a strong goal-oriented work ethic, and who have been driven by the words, *commitment, discipline, responsibility,* and *activism*. It is not that these things are bad. In fact, they are very important in human life, and never more needed than today. However, they need to be given their proper place, and should not be allowed to get in the way of the spiritual quest of silent, expectant waiting.

It was Howard Thurman who first helped me to understand the importance of what he called "simmering" on one's spiritual quest. "When traveling in the United States he always took trains because he felt that airplanes destroyed the rhythms of his spirit," writes Sam Keen about Thurman. "His rule of life . . . was to savor his time. 'Simmering' he called it. 'When you wake up in the morning,' he told me, 'never get out of bed—simmer. And when you get into bed at night, never go to sleep—simmer'" (*Fire in the Belly*).

Simmering. I love that term. Much to the dismay of Howard Thurman, I am sure, it has been in the airplane where I have learned to simmer best. A few years ago I was on a flight from Houston to Dallas, Texas, when suddenly, without warning, the plane hit an air pocket and was thrust downward. For a few brief moments there was panic on the plane, and the general sense that we were going to crash. It all happened very quickly, but within that short time of havoc, I came to terms with my own death. I was not in control. There was absolutely nothing that I could do to change the situation. If we went down, we went down, and it would be left to the National Transportation and Safety Board to find out *why*.

Ever since this experience, I have not had to use one tablet for air sickness. Before this time I could single-handedly keep the makers of such air-sick products operative for years! Now, the airplane has become one of those sacred places in my hurried life where I have learned to simmer best. Why? I am not in control of my environment, and I have come to terms with my own demise. As a result, I can relinquish my life totally and completely to God.

. . .

ENCOUNTER AND WITHDRAWAL

He withdrew to the wilderness and prayed.
—LUKE 5:16

When I served as the director of the Yokefellow Institute, an ecumenical center for retreats and continuing education, primarily for religious leaders, I would often lead conferences for clergy. One particular gathering stands out for the openness and honesty with which these pastors talked about the chaos into which they had been thrown as a result of the emotional and spiritual fatigue in their lives. As they gathered in the meeting room, they seemed to be genuinely enjoying one another's company. The program's focus for the next few days was to be on "Stress in the Ministry," and the quiet and peaceful surroundings of the back campus of Earlham College were already providing a healing influence for the conference attenders. As we sat together in that beautiful room overlooking the rolling hills of central Indiana, the participants began to share how they were feeling about their ministry, both spiritually and emotionally. Since it was an interdenominational group, and the participants had not known one another before they had arrived, there was considerable freedom to be honest about what they were feeling in their work.

One by one these pastors began to share their life stories—their call to ministry, the churches which they had served, and how they were feeling now. What soon became the operative word for this session together was "burnout." Burnout has been described as continuing to go through the motions of life, while the soul has departed. This certainly seemed true of this group. All had been pastors long enough to feel the frustration and know the difficulties of serving a local congregation. For the most part these were "mainline" pastors who were experiencing the pressures of the last decade of both numerical and financial decline, as well as the other cultural and societal pressures which all pastors are feeling as they seek to do ministry in an often chaotic world. Some were ready to leave the ministry for other work; some were looking for new pastorates, hoping that a change in geography would boost their sagging spirits, and some were just going to "tough it out" until retirement. All were spiritually and emotionally tired.

The shared experiences of these religious leaders can be multiplied throughout the spiritual landscape. These experiences are not necessarily debilitating, but they are detrimental to personal health and stifle ministerial effectiveness. They rob us of the spiritual vitality that inspires and excites us.

In an effort to understand such fatigue and the chaos phenomenon out of which it is produced, I have been helped by studying the pattern of life modeled by Jesus. Throughout the Gospels we discover a pattern of *encounter* with the world, and then *withdrawal* from the world for spiritual revitalization. What becomes apparent from reading about the life of Jesus is that he understood his effectiveness in the world to be directly related to his spiritual condition. The examples are numerous:

> And after he had dismissed the crowds, he went up on the mountain by himself to pray. (Matt. 14:23)

> And in the morning, a great while before day, he rose and went out to a lonely place, and there he prayed. (Mark 1:35)

> Perceiving then that they were about to come and take him by force to make him king, Jesus withdrew to the mountain by himself. (John 6: 15)

> But so much more the report went abroad concerning him; and great multitudes gathered to hear and to be healed of their infirmities. But he withdrew to the wilderness and prayed. (Luke 5:15–16)

This last text is especially meaningful for religious leaders who carry the burden of activity to the point of workaholism, for it shows that when Jesus was needed most, he "withdrew to the wilderness."

Although much has changed since the time of Jesus, the human condition is still basically the same. The encounters with the world, if anything, have increased. What seems to be needed in the modern world, where there is so much chaos swirling around us, is a contemporary understanding of "wilderness" and what such wilderness experiences of withdrawal would mean for spiritual revitalization—and not just for religious leaders, but for everyone who faces on a daily basis, confrontation in the world, i.e., *all of us*. Alvin Toffler was able to address this concern when he suggested in his book, *Future*

Shock, that we might develop enclaves of peace and quiet, representative of an earlier, more relaxed time, where we can, quite literally, get off of the world for a while, and become renewed. And yet, environment is only one dimension of the spiritual response to burnout.

In exploring prayer in the experience of chaos, a contemporary understanding of "wilderness" and its relationship to spiritual renewal would be helpful if creatively formed. The discipline of time applies here. I know how easy it is to say, "I don't have the time," and to use this excuse for not taking "time away" from my normal, daily routine in order to face my spiritual crisis. Such times away, I now know, are what make our daily activities meaningful. Walks in the park, a weekend at the coast, a quiet time in a corner of the house where eyes can be closed and meditation can be practiced—all contribute to the recovery of the spiritual dimension in our lives. To experience the rhythm of encounter and withdrawal as practiced by Jesus, is to learn the secret of abundant living. And, we are told in Scripture, we are not only to have life, but have it *abundantly.*

• • •

A TRANSFORMING VEHICLE

*The most awful, living, reverent frame I ever felt or beheld,
I must say, was his in prayer.*
— WILLIAM PENN ABOUT GEORGE FOX

It was a different kind of conference for me, to be sure. Most of the participants were sociologists, psychologists, criminologists, and judges. I was the lone theologian. As the vice-president of the International Institute for Youth, I had been asked to moderate a panel discussion on the topic, "Dimensions of a Program to Foster Cross-Cultural Research and Dissemination of Findings." It was the kind of program that academics love.

At the luncheon following this discussion I sat between the chairman of the Department of Sociology at the University of Southern California and a professor in the School of Social Work at the University of Pittsburgh. Across from me was a brilliant sociologist from the Netherlands who had made juvenile justice issues the focus of her research. In the course of the conversation, I turned to the sociologist from Los Angeles and said that I had recently read that there had been a substantial decrease in the homicide rate in Los Angeles County during the time of the 1988 Olympics, and that this was a shocking turnaround since they usually average about fifty homicides per week. I continued by saying that the author claimed that *prayer* had played a vital role in this reduction. I explained how there had been small prayer groups activated throughout the neighborhoods around the city, praying for a peaceful Olympics, and that it appeared to have some impact. Unfortunately, I caught the professor with something in his mouth, and he could barely keep his composure without choking while he laughed. Before long the whole table had erupted at what seemed to be the most laughable statement any of them had heard in a very long time. Prayer contributing to a change in the homicide rate of a city? *Preposterous.* At least that is what they thought.

"But above all he excelled in prayer." This statement from William Penn about George Fox would be difficult for many in our modern world to understand. It would be much easier to understand if Fox had "excelled" in sociology or psychology. He didn't. He excelled in prayer. These words are a part of a larger statement by Penn in his introduction to Fox's *Journal* about what he considered the most important characteristic of the founder of the people called Quakers. Penn continues: "The inwardness and weight of his spirit, the reverence and solemnity of his address and behavior, the fewness and fullness of his words, have often struck even strangers with admiration, as they used to reach others with consolation." And then Penn concludes his portrait of Fox with these words: "The most awful, living, reverent frame I ever felt or beheld, I must say, was his in prayer" (*The Rise and Progress of the People Called Quakers*).

George Fox believed in the power of prayer. He explored prayer in its many different dimensions. Out of the chaos of his earthly journey, he discovered prayer to be a centering influence, which he experienced as transformational—for individuals and groups of individuals. His own life was a witness to this transforming power.

The most striking thing that we know about this world is that it is inhabited by human beings, and the most important thing we know about these human beings is that they are forever in quest of making connection with the living God. It is the finite in search of union with the Infinite, and *prayer* is the transforming vehicle in this search. What is more noble than the human quest to make contact with the living God? I can think of none greater. And, what is more meaningful in human life than God's quest to make contact with us? Nothing.

It may never be said of you or me that the "most awful, living, reverent frame I ever beheld" was John or Jane Doe in prayer. It can be said, however, that out of the chaos of our lives the exploration of prayer can become an important part of our quest for spiritual intimacy. Jesus believed in the transformational component of prayer. And whether it be in an individual or the city of Los Angeles, prayer can be experienced as transforming. We are told in Scripture, and via the experiences of persons throughout the centuries, that through the healing power of prayer the lame have been known to walk again, the deaf have received the gift of hearing, and the blind have received sight. Out of chaos, a transforming experience through prayer is possible, and much to the dismay of my sociologist colleague, I believe it is even possible in Southern California.

• • •

PASSAGES INTO THE ETERNAL

I am not the man I was.
— EBENEZER SCROOGE

We cannot experience the Infinite in prayer and not be transformed by such a meeting, and we cannot experience spiritual transformation without the exploration of prayer forever becoming a central discipline in our lives. Both are intertwined and issue in glimpses, or passages into the eternal. In a time when so much is written about "faith development," I love reading or hearing about the "flashes of light" from heaven, which transformed Saul to Paul, or the exclamation, "I am not the man I was," which brings to culmination the transformation of Ebenezer Scrooge in Charles Dickens' *A Christmas Story.*

History is filled with stories of such passages into the eternal. There was the moment when George Fox, who "excelled in prayer," heard a voice which said, "There is one, even Christ Jesus, who can speak to thy condition," and as a result, Fox 's chaotic spiritual struggle was moved to a new dimension. John Wesley, the father of the "Methodist Movement" heard Martin Luther's *Commentary on Romans* being read, and his heart was "strangely warmed." The mathematician and philosopher, Blaise Pascal, wrote about his transformation, which was dated November 23, 1654: "From about half past ten in the evening until about half past twelve, FIRE. God of Abraham, God of

Isaac, God of Jacob, not of philosophers and scholars. Certitude, certitude, feeling, joy, peace . . . Let me never be separated from him. He is preserved only by the ways taught in the Gospel. Renunciation, total and sweet."

These are representative of moments when, out of chaos, God was confrontational with the human condition, and through the exploration of prayer, the "human condition" was also confrontational with God. As a result, these lives moved in an entirely different direction, and consequently, our lives are different as well. These are the moments in chaos, when the rest of life is given meaning. While we are in them or as we reflect upon them, they define for us *who* we are, and *where* we are going. Hopefully, we will also be better equipped on *how* to get there.

In the Greek, these are referred to as *kairos* moments, i.e., a *special* time, moments when God breaks through and newness happens. These *kairos* times are much more likely to happen in chaos, when we are moved by the circumstances in life out of our comfortable routine, ritual, and patterns of seeming contentment. Whatever the occasion for such *kairos* moments, whether pure pain or pure joy, we become more available and open for the God of transformation to enter our lives in new and exciting ways, and a passage into the eternal opens before us. It is interesting that the Chinese character for *chaos* and *opportunity* is one and the same.

Thomas Moore knows about this spiritual truth. In *Care of the Soul*, he writes:

> Care of the soul—appreciates the mystery of human suffering and does not offer the illusion of a problem-free life. It sees every fall into ignorance and confusion as an opportunity to discover that the beast residing (at the center of one's dark night) is also an angel. . . . To approach this paradoxical

point of tension where adjustment and abnormality meet is to move closer to the realization of our mystery-filled, star born nature.

During a counseling session this past year I was confronted with this kind of transformational paradigm. A woman came to my office and told me that she had just experienced the worst year of her life. She had been in an automobile accident, breaking her arm and receiving numerous lacerations. Her mother had just died prior to the accident, and her job was being phased out. On top of all of this, she discovered that her best friend was having an affair with her husband. In the midst of the tears, she looked up and said, "You know, Jim, this has been the worst year of my life." And then pausing, she added, "But I would not trade it for anything because of the intense and accelerated spiritual growth I have been experiencing."

Out of chaos we can give birth to dancing stars. In the midst of crises, passages into the eternal can open before us. The following passages are helpful signposts in our own quest for spiritual intimacy, beginning with the beautiful words found in the *Journal* of Katharine Mansfield, as she struggled with tuberculosis:

> Everything in life that we really accept undergoes a change so suffering must become love. This is the mystery. This is what I must do. I must pass from personal love to greater love. . . . It is to lose oneself more utterly, to love more deeply, to feel oneself part of life—not separate. Oh life! accept me—make me worthy, teach me. I write that. I look up. The leaves move in the garden, the sky is pale, and I catch myself weeping. It is hard—it is hard to make a good death.

A business man from Detroit went with one of the Ministry of Money groups (founded by the Church of the Savior in Washington, D.C.) to Calcutta, India. When he arrived back home, he wrote a letter about his transformational experience while there, which included the passage below. Mary Cosby of the Church of the Savior in Washington, D.C., first shared this story at the Annual Yokefellow Conference in 1989:

> I must tell you that Calcutta was the most depressing place I have ever been in my entire life, but I would go back tomorrow if I could for the life-changing experience that happened to me there. I was feeding a little brown old man who was covered with maggots and sores. He was too weak to sit up. I accidentally spilled some rice on his neck, and at first I thought I would die if I had to touch him. But I had to get the hot rice off his neck, and so I finally risked touching him.
>
> When I touched him, all heaven broke loose! I couldn't believe it! He began to speak and to smile, and to wiggle his head in that peculiar Indian way. Though I couldn't understand the words, the body language was unmistakable. He was overwhelmed with a touch. The feeding continued for some time, and what I wasn't prepared for was something happening to me. A big childish, irrepressible grin came over my face. I'd almost forgotten that such feelings existed. Joy seemed to flow between him and me as we looked at each other.
>
> I realized that up to this point in my preparation for this trip, I had focused on the suffering of the poor, and on trying to identify with Jesus when I worked with the sufferings of these poor. But here I was being confronted with an experience of pure joy that seemed to contradict everything I'd been told or experienced. If, indeed, I had met the Jesus of suffering in this man, I had also met the Jesus of abundant joy.
>
> I went back later because I couldn't bear not to see him one more time. I didn't even know whether he was

still alive. He was asleep and I was glad he was alive, because I looked down on him and said, "Thank you good friend, I owe you everything because you have reawakened in me my thirst for joy."

In his *Journals*, Søren Kierkegaard writes about "that tragic, ruthless glance" of desperation which can move one into the eternal:

And this is the simple truth: that to live is to feel oneself lost. He who accepts it has already begun to find himself, to be on firm ground. Instinctively, as do the shipwrecked, he will look around for something to which to cling; and that tragic, ruthless glance, absolutely sincere because it is a question of his salvation, will cause him to bring order into the chaos of his life.

The seventeenth-century Quaker, Mary Penington, tells of giving up "my whole strength" as she was transformed in her house at Chalfont in England:

But oh! the joy that filled my soul in the first meeting ever held in our house at Chalfont. To this day I have a fresh remembrance of it. It was then the Lord enabled me to worship him in that which was undoubtedly his own, and give up my whole strength, yea to swim in the life which overcame me that day.

Oh! long had I desired to worship him with acceptation, and lift up my hands without doubting, which I witnessed that day in that assembly. I acknowledged his great mercy and wonderful kindness; for I could say, "This is it which I have longed and waited for, and feared I never should have experienced." (*Experiences in the Life of Mary Penington*)

On his death-bed, James Nayler spoke these, his last words:

There is a spirit which I feel that delights to do no evil, nor to revenge any wrong, but delights to endure all things, in hope to enjoy its own in the end. Its hope is to outlive all wrath and contention, and to weary out all exaltation and cruelty, or whatever is of a nature contrary to itself. It sees to the end of all temptations. As it bears no evil in itself, so it conceives none in thoughts to any other. If it be betrayed, it bears it, for its ground and spring is the mercies and forgiveness of God. Its crown is meekness, its life is everlasting love unfeigned; it takes its kingdom with entreaty and not with contention, and keeps it by lowliness of mind.

In God alone it can rejoice, though none else regard it, or can own its life. It's conceived in sorrow, and brought forth without any to pity it, nor doth it murmur at grief and oppression. It never rejoiceth but through sufferings; for with the world's joy it is murdered. I found it alone, being forsaken. I have fellowship therein with them who lived in dens and desolate places in the earth, who through death obtained this resurrection and eternal holy life. (*There Is a Spirit*)

In her book about her husband, *A Man Called Peter*, Catherine Marshall writes about one of the lessons learned by Peter while he was hospitalized for a heart-attack. It came in response to a question posed by a minister friend from Maryland: "I'm curious to know something," the minister began. "What did you learn during your illness?" "Do you really want to know?" Peter answered promptly. "I learned that the Kingdom of God goes on without Peter Marshall."

The following experience relates to the death of his son Lowell at the age of eleven, while Rufus Jones was on a voyage to England in 1903. It is found in his book, *The Luminous Trail*:

The night before landing in Liverpool I awoke in my berth with a strange sense of trouble and sadness. As I lay wondering what it meant, I felt myself invaded by a Presence and held by Everlasting Arms. It was the most extraordinary experience I had ever had. But I had no intimation that anything was happening to Lowell. When we landed in Liverpool a cable informed me that he was desperately ill, and a second cable, in answer to one from me, brought the dreadful news that he was gone. When the news reached my friend John Wilhelm Rowntree, he experienced a profound sense of Divine Presence enfolding him and me, and his comfort and love were an immense help to me in my trial. . . . I know now, as I look back across the years, that nothing has carried me up into the life of God, or done more to open out the infinite meaning of love, than the fact that love can span this break of separation, can pass beyond the visible and hold right on across the chasm. The mystic union has not broken and knows no end.

The transformation of the writer/journalist, Malcolm Muggeridge, from agnostic to committed Christian was not a sudden experience, but occurred over many years, in brief encounters with *kairos* moments. His testimony is heart-warming, and in this passage he reflects on his "former life" and where his pilgrimage has led. It is found in his book, *A Twentieth-Century Testimony* :

When I look back on my life nowadays, which I sometimes do, what strikes me most forcibly about it is that what seemed at the time most significant and seductive, seems now most futile and absurd. For instance, success in all of its various guises; being known and being praised; ostensible pleasures, like acquiring money or seducing women, or traveling, going to and fro in the world and up and down in it like Satan, exploring and experiencing whatever Vanity Fair has to offer.

In retrospect all these exercises in self-gratification seem pure fantasy, what Pascal called "licking the earth."

They are diversions designed to distract our attention from the true purpose of our existence in this world, which is, quite simply, to look for God, and, in looking, to find Him, and, having found Him, to love Him, thereby establishing a harmonious relationship with His purposes for His creation.

In the passage which follows, we learn about the transformational importance of the less traveled road in the life of Robert Frost:

> He wasn't really happy with the direction his life was headed. He pondered leaving his teaching position to embark upon the career of poet. Would it be madness? As he reflected on his life, the woods were silent. Suddenly he noticed a man walking at a distance. He watched as the man seemed to pause and consider two roads. The man chose the less traveled road and disappeared from sight.
>
> The young teacher was transformed by sudden insight. Quickly he returned to civilization, resigned his teaching post, and embarked on the risky venture of poetry. Within two years of that decision he felt compelled to write a poem articulating his experience which has become a classic in American literature, "The Road Not Taken." It had made all the difference to Robert Frost. (*Quaker Life*, June, 1993)

We cannot *think* our way into an experience with the living God, but we can *cultivate* the expectancy of such transformational moments . . . in silence and patient waiting . . . in savoring the beauty of the creation . . . by paying attention to our dreams . . . in our relationships with others, in short by exploring prayer in all of its many and varied dimensions. And, as we live within the expectant rhythms of such God transforming moments, our chaos can be made sacred.

4

Dancing with Paradox

The deeper we get into reality, the more numerous will
be the questions we cannot answer.
— BARON FRIEDRICH VON HUGEL

Life has many different dimensions. If we are growing at all, the older we become, the more dimensions we will discover. We become less sure of our certainties, and find ourselves saying, "But on the other hand . . ." and "Yes, but . . .," a lot more. In the experience of chaos, paradox will be a more frequent dance partner, for we will discover that two truths, in apparent contradiction, may be the only way that we can explain what we are experiencing. Learning how to dance with paradox in the quest for spiritual intimacy, helps to make our chaos sacred.

A careful reading of Scripture will demonstrate how much of the Christian faith is paradoxical, and how Jesus emerges as the chief proponent of such a paradoxical faith. The Kingdom of God, Jesus tells us, is something great, and yet it is compared to a little mustard seed. The Kingdom, we are told, is something pure, and yet it is compared to a woman, who, in Gospel times, was considered impure. Further, such a Kingdom is a place where the poor are blessed; the first are last; in weakness we are made strong; the humble are exalted, and the proud are humbled. *Paradox.*

As I have traveled on my spiritual journey through chaos, six major paradoxes have emerged, which have helped me to clarify the complexities of human nature and the world in which we live. There are, of course, many more, but out of my experience and spiritual quest, the following have become dominant.

• • •

THE PARADOX OF SEPARATION AND CONNECTION

God plucks the world out of our hearts, loosening the chains of attachment. And he hurls the world into our hearts, where we and God together carry it in infinitely tender love.
— THOMAS KELLY

The more detached from this world we become, the more intensely we are connected to it. I have *felt* the truth of this paradox. Feeling detached from the world is not a new experience for me, since I have always considered myself somewhat of an observer within my outer environment—*just passing through*, thank you. And yet, out of this experience of separation, there are moments of real connectedness, when I look into the eyes of fellow pilgrims and see the Inner Light of God burning within them, or when I hear about the people suffering within a war-torn or poverty-stricken country, and my heart reaches out to them. There is a strangeness of feeling in this dance of separation and connectedness which is paradoxical.

As we experience chaos enveloping us, withdrawing from the world is a natural response. Friends and acquaintances that we knew prior to the chaos no longer feed or energize our spirits, and the work which we used to love loses its meaning. The new compact disc player or computer that medicated our pain for a while does not fill the emptiness we are feeling. We begin to feel numb to all that is happening around us.

As the familiar attachments to this world are loosening, and as the chaos intensifies, new experiences of attachment begin to dawn. But this time they are *spiritual* attachments, with love at the core. It is a love for all persons and experiences, seeking to learn, through each soul with whom we connect and each experience we have, how God is working. We move from a place of feeling power and control over the world, to allowing God to move in us and through us, connecting us to the world in new, spiritual ways. Rather than feeling dominant over one another, we learn that we are all equal travelers on a spiritual journey—regardless of station or position in life, as the world would have us judge one another. Instead of using the world for gain and profit, we allow the world to use us, sensitizing us to our interconnectedness with all living things. In practical terms, this means that we no longer stand in judgment over those, who, we used to feel, did not quite measure up to our expectations or social standing. All artificial, human-made barriers, be it race or wealth, no longer apply. All persons, from the homeless to the most materially comfortable, tug at our hearts in a penetrating love of one for another. It is a love born out of nonjudgmentalism and acceptance. And, life can never be the same as it was before the new feelings of spiritual intimacy and chaos broke upon us.

Being separated from the world and yet more attached to it, leads us to a new appreciation of the many dimensions of love. To carry the world in our hearts, growing in empathy and interconnectedness, we become open to new ways of relating to one another. We all seek love, and love also seeks us. Although we feel connected to all, loving in new ways, there are still special soul-mates who move us into dimensions of loving never before experienced. What a beautiful gift such soul-mates are to our journey! They may only travel with us for a brief season, or connect with us for a lifetime, but however long they are in our lives, we are never the same for having known them. All relationships are spiritual at the core, but the *degree* to which we experience the spiritual with one another will vary. To be spiritually sensitive to each experience and relationship along our journey, will open us to new and wonderful possibilities for growth and love which would not have been open to us before entering chaos.

No one lived the paradox of separation and connection more fully than the eighteenth-century Quaker, John Woolman. Few writings have meant more to me over the years than *The Journal of John Woolman*. In this journal, Woolman tells about his life, travels, and ever deepening social conscience—separating from the world, but ever more connected to it. It was Charles Lamb who said, "Get the writings of John Woolman by heart." "By heart" is really the only way to "get" the writings of Woolman, or to understand the paradox of separation and connection. They defy the world's traditional reason.

There is a certain passage in the journal which has always moved me deeply. It has to do with Woolman's description of his own transformation process as he became detached from the world, and yet ever more intensely connected to it. It begins with the words,

> While I silently ponder on that change wrought in me, I find no language equal to it nor any means to convey to another a clear idea of it. I looked upon the works of God in this visible creation and an awfulness covered me; my heart was tender and often contrite, and a universal love to my fellow creatures increased in me. This will be understood by such who have trodden in the same path. Some glances of real beauty may be seen in their faces who dwell in true meekness. There is a harmony in the sound of that voice to which

divine love gives utterance. . . . Yet all these do not fully show forth that inward life to such who have felt it.

The major attraction of Woolman for me is that he did not just *talk* about being transformed, nor did his transformation last for just a few days or weeks. Instead, it was a transformation he lived, day in and day out, until his untimely death from smallpox at the age of fifty-two.

As we seek to understand the spiritual workings of the paradox of separation and connection, we are helped by studying the marks of Woolman's spiritual transformation. The *first* clearly discernible mark was his *entry into the fellowship of suffering*. In his journal, Woolman shares a dream he had which moved him to recognize that it was impossible to be separated from the pain and death of others:

> I was brought so near the gates of death, that I forgot my name. Being then desirous to know who I was, I saw a mass of matter of a dull and gloomy color, between the south and the east, and was informed that this mass was human beings, in as great misery as they could be, and live, and that *I was mixed in with them, and henceforth I might not consider myself as a distinct or separate being.*

Because Woolman felt so interconnected with the suffering and the poor, he lived his life in such sensitivity that he refused to wear dyed clothing because of the slave labor used to make the dyes, and when he traveled to England he went by steerage where the poorest of the poor traveled in the ship. And such fellowship with the suffering extended to the animal kingdom as well, finding expression in his refusal to travel by coach because of the cruelty rendered upon the horses forced to meet demanding time schedules. An experience in his youth contributed to this sensitivity. Writing in his journal he tells about how he once killed a mother robin with a stone:

> I beheld her lying dead and thought those young ones for
> which she was so careful must now perish for want of their
> dam to nourish them; and after some painful consideration
> on the subject, I climbed up the tree, took all the young birds
> and killed them, supposing that better than to leave them to
> pine away and die miserably. . . . I then went on my errand,
> but for some hours could think of little else but the cruelties
> I had committed, and was much troubled.

A second element of Woolman's transformation can be described as *a profound simplicity* in his faith. Woolman struggled long and hard with the difficult issues associated with the faith by which he sought to live. Early in his life he was confused about his relationship with God, living, as he called it, from "one youthful vanity to another." As he matured spiritually, however, he seemed to be able to work through the more cumbersome issues surrounding his beliefs, and by remaining close to what he called "inner promptings," he was able to live in a close, yet simple relationship with God.

In many ways, Woolman reminds one of Mother Teresa of Calcutta. Her good friend, Malcolm Muggeridge once told me the story of a time when Mother Teresa was invited to be on a television program with a panel of Christian leaders discussing their faith. Here was the archbishop of Canterbury and other world renowned theologians, and then there was Mother Teresa. When asked to explain her faith, following the very eloquent dissertations of the other guests, who could be very impressive academically, Mother Teresa said, "Oh, I try to follow the example of Jesus. I just want to love as Jesus would have me love—care for the sick, feed the hungry, and love the poor."

Following the program, the archbishop was heard to say, "You know, if I had to spend much time with that woman, I would be in real trouble!" The "trouble" which this simplicity of faith causes is that when we are in the presence of such powerful examples of Christlikeness as a Woolman or Mother Teresa, we experience the discomfort of knowing how far *we* are from such a spirituality. It is a childlike openness to the workings of the living God. It is not a simplistic faith, but a faith of profound simplicity.

Throughout Woolman's transformation, he moved into *an ever deepening humility*. His last missionary journey was to England in 1772. He arrived in London after five weeks in the steerage of a boat, crossing the Atlantic. He barely had enough time to reach Devonshire House where London Yearly Meeting of Friends was beginning their sessions. His entrance was clearly startling to the well-groomed London Friends— wearing his undyed clothing and looking quite rumpled. After stating how he was led by God to minister among English Friends, one Friend stood and said, "Perhaps John Woolman might feel that his dedication of himself to this service was accepted, without further labor, and that he might now feel free to return home to America." Since Woolman was such a sensitive man, recognizing that these were cruel words, he was moved to tears, openly weeping in the midst of the sessions of London Yearly Meeting. Following a period of silence, John Woolman arose and stated that he was not yet led to return home, and then delivered a most moving sermon, convincing all present of the authenticity of his vocation. At the conclusion, the very man who had spoken so cruelly, making the harsh suggestion that Woolman return home, arose and said his doubts were gone, and that John Woolman should feel free to stay among English Friends as long as he was led to do so.

Always, John Woolman was testing his inner promptings from God within his faith community. He was bold in his concern for social justice, yet humble and tender in expressing this concern, always in humility, seeking what God would have him do, in the company of one another. He was a living example of the paradox of separation and connection.

• • •

THE PARADOX OF SPIRITUAL GROWTH AND HUMILITY

We may as well think to see without eyes or live without breath, as
to live in the spirit of religion without the spirit of humility.
— WILLIAM LAW

The more we grow spiritually, the further from spiritual per-fection we realize we are. On this important point of humility, all of the evidence of the ages agrees. With each step of growth, we are opened to new possibilities of growth, of which, in the end, there is no end.

Chaos can accelerate spiritual growth, and, consequent-ly, the recognition of how much more we need to grow. In chaos we are out of control and on shaky ground, when the pil-lars of former beliefs are crashing down all around us. It is a time for turning inward, where we can gather our spiritual resources. We reach inside to the God within for support and comfort, for all else seems to be crumbling.

A few weeks ago I was on a spiritual high, feeling myself grow by leaps and bounds. I felt good inside, outside, upside, and downside. A smile stretched across my face from ear to ear, and even the most discouraging news could not put me into a funk. I wrote relatives and asked them to contribute to their favorite charities rather than purchase Christmas gifts for me. I was reading volumes of devotional classics, constantly under-lining and writing "YES" in the margins. In the darkest of rooms you could almost see the Inner Light of God glowing within me. I felt as though God and I were ONE.

Slowly, hour by hour and day by day, I began to lose, sepa-rate, or fall back from what I had experienced at the height of this spiritual encounter. I struggled to keep it. I prayed more intensely; read more ardently; contributed to charities more generously, but I could not retain what I felt so strongly just a few days ago. Alas, most of the normalcy of life returned and much of the routine of daily living, once again, became *routinized*.

What happened? I have since reflected on this experience, and have likened it to a walk on the beach with God. I envisioned the spiritual "high" as the discovery of a perfectly shaped sand dollar. There it was in all of its beauty. I stopped and built a sand castle around it, hoping to protect it from its environment. Soon, however, the waves were lapping at the edges of the protective wall, and I could not hold back the onslaught of the tide. I looked up to discover that God was walking up ahead, and had not stopped. I started to walk again, but strained my neck to keep looking back at the sand dollar. Pretty soon it was out of sight, and I had to turn my head forward, to the possibility of *new* sand dollar discoveries. The beauty of the sand dollar is still in my heart's memory, but I now know that there are new ones to discover—new spiritual experiences to be had, for transformation is a continual process of discovering new sand dollars.

This experience has become one of those nodal moments in my life. How human it is to want to stop, build a shrine, frame and hang on the wall, write a creed, or otherwise hold on to forever and ever an experience with God. It cannot be done, except in memory, for spiritual growth is fluid and there is always more to learn and to discover.

• • •

THE PARADOX OF MATURITY AND WISDOM

. . . an adult is not the highest stage of development. The end
cycle is that of the independent, clear-minded, all-seeing child
that is the level known as wisdom.

— BEN HOFF

The more enlightened we become as adults, the more child-like will be our wisdom. Jesus said, "Let the little children come unto me," and that we must become like children to enter the Kingdom of heaven. Writing in *The Tao of Pooh*, Ben Hoff says, "Why do the enlightened seem filled with light and happiness like children? Why do they sometimes look and even talk like children? Because they are." In his novel, *By the River Piedra I Sat Down and Wept*, Paulo Coelho reminds his readers that "human wisdom is madness in the eyes of God. But if we listen to the child who lives in our soul, our eyes will grow bright. If we do not lose contact with that child, we will not lose contact with life."

One way to remain in contact with the child within us, is to read the classics of children's literature, such as *Winnie the Pooh*, *Charlotte's Web*, and *The Velveteen Rabbit*, all of which offer profound spiritual insights. Such stories are the lifeline to dreams and imagination, without which we would cease to be fully human. They are word pictures which are attempts to grasp the *why* of life so that we can more fully live into the *how*. Within such stories resides the recognition that the most difficult issues of life are paradoxical and mysterious. Few writings are more spiritually moving than the following from *The Velveteen Rabbit* by Margery Williams Bianco:

> "What is REAL?" asked the Rabbit one day. "Does it mean having things that buzz inside you and a stick-out handle?"
>
> "Real isn't how you are made," said the Skin Horse. "It's a thing that happens to you. When a child loves you for a long, long time, not just to play with, but REALLY loves you, then you become Real."
>
> "Does it hurt?"
>
> "Sometimes." For he was always truthful. "When you are Real you don't mind being hurt."

"Does it happen all at once, like being wound up, or bit by bit?"

"It doesn't happen all at once. You become. It takes a long time. That's why it doesn't often happen to people who break easily, or who have sharp edges, or who have to be carefully kept. Generally, by the time you are Real, most of your hair has been loved off, and your eyes drop out and you get loose in the joints and very shabby. But these things don't matter at all, because once you are Real you can't be ugly, except to people who don't understand . . . "

Children delight in mystery and follow their hearts. Children know that there is still a lot to know and to discover, and that the more they learn and discover, there is more to learn and to discover. They are perpetual askers of questions and love the process of seeking. The paradox of maturity and wisdom is born out of chaos.

. . .

The Paradox of Knowing and Mystery

For when I came into the silent assemblies of God's people,
I felt a secret power among them.
— ROBERT BARCLAY

If we are to know the Living God, we must be comfortable with mystery. No matter how much we seek to define God and "systematize" our process of knowing (Is there anything more absurd than the term "systematic theology"?), there will always be mystery beyond our knowledge.

And yet we are constantly about the task of erasing mystery and trying to define God within the well-structured boundaries of our limited understanding. We want laws to follow and guard against our "sinful nature," and so we define God as primarily a law-giver. We put God in legalistic terms as one who gives endless lists of commandments, whose primary requirement is blind obedience, and who is satisfied if we follow inflexible rituals which lack inner meaning. Or, we set forth a static interpretation of God by limiting God to what is found in the Bible. This produces a "bibliolatry," i.e., a worship of the book, rather than the One to Whom the book points.

Ultimately, to know God and to be comfortable in mystery means that we begin with our own *experience*. Such experience cannot be programmed, diagrammed, or formulated. It comes in openness, receptivity, and trust. We experience God in relationships, quiet communion, and in everyday life, with all of its foibles, hardships, and chaos.

I was a young boy when I first heard the words of the seventeenth-century theologian Robert Barclay. Sitting in the silence of the Minneapolis Friends Meeting, I heard my father repeat the following words many times as he spoke out of the silence:

> For when I came into the silent assemblies of God's people, I felt a secret power among them, which touched my heart, and as I gave way unto it I found the evil weakening in me and the good raised up.

The transforming power of Barclay's testimony can still bring tears to my eyes. And the first part of his confession is just as moving:

> Not by strength of arguments or by a particular disquisition of each doctrine and convincement of my understanding thereby, came I to receive and bear witness of the Truth, but by being secretly reached by the Life. (*The Apology*)

Secretly reached by the Life . . . in the silent assemblies of God's people. Barclay uses the term *secret* or *secretly* twice in this brief depiction of his experience. It seems an odd use of the word *secret*, and yet it is, perhaps, the only way he could describe what had touched his soul so profoundly. It is to admit to the awesome mystery of God. It was not the kind of mystery or secret associated with a God who loomed high above the human race in a faraway heaven, but, instead, a "secret power" which was *felt* in this earthly realm, and which could actually move one to *feel* "the evil weakening" and "the good raised up."

During a recent meeting a woman asked me: "How do you define *spiritual?*" As the minister of spiritual growth at Plymouth Church, it would seem to be an important definition to know. And yet, for me, the word is elusive and impossible to define fully. This mysterious quality cannot be disregarded, and I hope that the word will always elude capture and exact definition. We need such words in our human vocabulary—words that are always just beyond our grasp, in a region where we travel more by faith than by sight. Whatever your opinion of the best-selling books, *Conversations with God*, we can agree with what the author purports God to say regarding words:

> Words are really the least effective communication. They are most open to misinterpretation. . . . Words are merely utterances: noises that stand for feelings, thoughts, and experience. They are symbols, signs, insignias. They are not Truth. Words may help you understand something. *Experience allows you to know.* (*Conversations with God*, Book 1)

Learning to be comfortable in the tension between knowing and mystery is to accept our human frailty and admit with the Apostle Paul that in this life we do, indeed, see through a glass darkly. The more we come to know the Living God, the more we will discover there is to know. Thus *mystery* becomes an important part of our quest for spiritual intimacy.

• • •
THE PARADOX OF ANSWERS AND QUESTIONS

*. . . be patient toward all that is unsolved in your heart and
try to love the questions themselves, like locked rooms and like
books that are written in a very foreign tongue. Do not now seek
the answers, which cannot be given you because you would not
be able to live them. And the point is, to live everything. Live the
questions now. Perhaps you will then gradually, without noticing
it, live along some distant day into the answer.*

— RAINER MARIA RILKE

As we seek answers within the chaos we are experiencing,
they may only be found in the questions we ask. In the discipline of reflective thought, we discover that questions can
be sacred.

In her Gifford Lectures, entitled, *The Life of the Mind*,
Hannah Arendt states that her interest in "mental activities"
had many sources, but was most immediately influenced by
the Eichmann trial in Jerusalem. In observing Eichmann
respond to questions, she wrote that he showed no evidence
of being able to "stop and think," but rather spoke in "cliché-
ridden language."

To "stop and think," and to examine our actions in a
reflective way as we interact within our various worlds of activity, are becoming less and less a part of our lives. "Cliché-rid-
den" language abounds, and although we may not experience
the demonic ways of Eichmann, we know something about the
thoughtlessness of his existence. Most of the generation which
more fully embraced the value of reflective examination is
passing, and the sight, sound, and action generation is becoming dominant. Thoughtlessness is everywhere in today's world,
the by-products being minds without rudders, floating in a sea

of confusion. And for many millions, religion, in the traditional sense, has failed to provide the necessary certainty to clarify the confusion.

Humans need to perceive ultimate certainty and meaning in life. We are very tough creatures in many respects, who can endure mental and physical torture over prolonged periods of time. One thing with which we cannot live, however, is the sense that our lives have no meaning—that there is no ultimate certainty and no reason for our existence on this earth.

In this human search for meaning, there is value in psychological and sociological reflection, for these disciplines *inform* our search. But they do not get at the core issue of the search and ask the question, "Why am I here?" This question of ultimate meaning cannot be discovered in the writings of Max Weber or Carl Jung, though they are helpful. To begin the pursuit of asking such reflective questions we must start within the realm of *theology*.

In each of the synoptic Gospels—Matthew, Mark, and Luke, there can be found an exchange between Jesus and the Pharisees, which helps us understand the importance of the theological task. The question asked of Jesus focused on what must be done to inherit eternal life. Jesus responded, "Love the Lord your God with all your heart and with all your soul and with all your strength and with all your *mind*, and your neighbor as yourself."

To love God with the mind leads to the reflective examination of one's life, and such examination leads to *questions*. The need for such examination can come at many chaos entry points in our lives—the result of human failure or tragedy, transition or triumph, or a deepening hunger to know and to be known by the living God. Whatever the impetus to such life examination, the consequence will be spiritual growth.

Søren Kierkegaard wrote of the "leap of faith" that one must take after letting theological inquiry and examination move us as far as they can. And yet today, many are taking the leap before they have adequately struggled with the "Why am I here?" question. Of course, life examination, study and thinking, and the pursuit of questions surrounding the issue of our life purpose are difficult. But the fruit of such questions is what makes life meaningful.

The healthy process of life examination and the faith questions surrounding such examination are under attack today by many who would prefer to make religious faith a closed affair—closed minds/closed hearts. There are those who believe that the questions of faith get in the way of ardent belief. They are *not* comfortable, in the words of Ranier Maria Rilke, to "Live the questions." And yet, sometimes the answers we seek are in the questions we ask.

We live in a world of mystery. Albert Schweitzer said, "The highest knowledge is to know that we are surrounded by mystery." To love the questions is to live within the mystery on the way to belief. Even Jesus in his most agonizing hour asked, "My God, my God *why* hast Thou forsaken me?" Knowing that Jesus felt free to question the mystery should encourage us to do the same. There are times in the chaos of life when it takes more courage to stand by one's reflective questions than to stand by beliefs which have not yet been tested by experience. And in the chaos, when all is open to question, *experience* is really all that we have. In the trustworthiness of religious experience lies the affirmation that seeking and questioning will eventually lead to finding . . . *and more questions*. In this spiritual context, *why* becomes a sacred word.

• • •

THE PARADOX OF LOVE

To find love, you must first find it in yourself. Then the
whole universe will mirror it back.
— MELODY BEATTIE

The more love we experience, the more love we must give away. We all seek love, and we are told that God is love. If there is a universal truth we all know experientially, it is that we all *want* to be loved. And yet love can only be ours if we give it away to others. The more we give, the greater is the return. Trying to control or possess love is like trying to hold onto a sunbeam. It cannot be done. In chaos, we lose the illusion of control and possession.

Giving love away is difficult. Many would rather opt for power and control than to give and receive love, and in the midst of the chaos in our lives, we try hard to retain power and control—to our spiritual detriment.

Jesus was tempted by power. The devil, we are told, offered Jesus the kingdoms of the world in all of their splendor. He said no. The temptation is real, and I am sure that Jesus must have been tempted, as we all would be. Henri Nouwen has said, "It seems easier to be God than to love God . . . to own life than to love life." Love is a threat to power and control. Jesus gave and received love freely, rejecting the temptation to power and control. He understood the paradox of love.

Dancing with paradox. It is in the chaos of our lives that we learn the steps to such a dance. At first we stumble and feel awkward, but as we grow and become more comfortable in our newness, the steps will become more natural. We can delight in separation and connection; growth and humility; maturity and wisdom; knowing and mystery; answers and questions, and love. Paradox is a gift, and in the recognition of such a gift, chaos becomes sacred.

5

Experiencing Pilgrimage

God is a richly related being whose innermost nature is in
his ceaseless participation and sharing.
— ALFRED NORTH WHITEHEAD

Within the chaos, God is evolving with us. The dramatic
scene where Moses confronts the burning bush and
asks, "Who are you, Lord?" is helpful in understanding this
God of process and journey. Most versions of Hebrew Scripture
indicate God's answer with the words, "I am," or "I am Who I
am" (Exod. 3:13–14). Thus God came to be known as the great
"I am." The original Hebrew, however, can be translated to
read, "I am BECOMING who I am BECOMING." This represents an evolutionary God who is still creating and evolving
with us. This is a God of Pilgrimage who is on a journey, and
who continues to act, forgive, create, and love. And, this God,
who is "a richly related being," is within us all, in "ceaseless
participation and sharing."

Pilgrimage is another one of those universal experiences
with unique consequences. "Everything is on its way somewhere," says George Malley (John Travolta) in the movie,
Phenomenon. And yet, each "way somewhere" is distinct to the

experience of the person or thing. At the heart of each one's pilgrimage is one's unique memory of experience.

• • •

THE SACRAMENT OF MEMORY
Not far downstream was a dry channel where the river had run once, and part of the way to come to know a thing is through its death. But years ago I had known the river when it flowed through the now dry channel, so I could enliven its stony remains with the waters of memory
— NORMAN MACLEAN

In his book, *To a Dancing God*, Sam Keen writes about an encounter with a man while Sam was constructing a redwood fence around his home. The man, who was walking his dog, stopped and watched Sam for a while, and then inquired if he could help. Sam told him he could, but before the conversation could go further, the man explained that he had been injured by a small piece of metal which had tore into his brain, lodging in the area which stores and controls memory. The man survived the accident, but it had left him with no control over his memory. There were times he could remember events which had just occured, and there were other times he could remember events from long ago. But he was unable to keep the two in balance. This lack of a dependable memory kept the man from employment and planning for the future. Because of this, he asked Sam to write his name and address on a piece of paper, which he could use to remind him of the encounter. Keen relates what happened next: "We planned to meet on the following Monday and work on the fence together but he never appeared. I imagine that he found the slip of paper on which I had written my name and address in his pocket and could not recall how it got there."

What are we without our memories? Each of us is shaped and molded by experiences which are unique to the individual. Without memories of those experiences, how do we define who we are? Our past weaves our present. Who we are today, and the experiences we encounter, will create tomorrow's possibilities. How tragic for the man whose memory was disturbed, for he is destined to never connect with anyone or anything— confined to a limbo of passing moments, without a history, and, consequently, without a future.

As we experience chaos, to *remember* becomes even more significant as a spiritual exercise. The word "remember" actually means to gather the memories together. *Remembering* makes us *whole*. Karla Minear writes:

> Because life is as full of tragedy as it is of joy and love, our memories will be bittersweet. But there is meaning in each bump and rough spot, each bend in the road. Only when we look back can we see the pattern of sunlight and shadow. When we are in the midst of the dailiness of life we often miss the hand of God painting the landscape. We fail to see the mystical way our lives unfold until later, when we have time to reflect and to remember. (*Quaker Life*, December, 1993)

A couple of years ago I began the process of "mining" my own personal mythology, reflecting and remembering. As a way to begin such an exercise, I went back to the old neighborhood which I had known as a boy, and slowly walked the streets. There are special places in everyone's life where you would like time to stand still. One such place for me is the neighborhood in which I grew up. For many in difficult home situations, "the neighborhood" is a source of stability. Each day brings many changes, but the old neighborhood is known territory. When I was growing up, I knew every alley, every yard, every tree, and every fence within a two-mile radius from my front door. I knew which opening in each fence I could pass my bike through, and which yards to avoid because of hostile adults or big dogs. There was a sense of security in knowing all of this. I knew that there was always one area of Muncie, Indiana, where my knowledge of the territory provided a safe place. Upon my return not all was the same. As with all of life, the passing of time brings change:

—The basketball court in Hannaford's driveway was completely overgrown with weeds, and the basketball goal atop the garage was falling apart. In the early and mid-'60s this was *the* place to be. Basketball in my neighborhood, as in most Indiana neighborhoods, was always the first choice of sport.

—The train tracks which ran behind my house were no longer there. It was a spur line of the Nickel Plate Road which went to the Schwartz Paper Company. I never hopped that little train, but many of my friends did. It was a dangerous form of excitement. I did put pennies on the track to be squashed by the passing train wheels. I still have a few of these mementos.

—The blackberry bush by the side of the road is gone. I remember eating blackberries until I was sick.

—Our next door neighbors, the Mayfields, had moved long ago. Dr. Mayfield was a history professor at Ball State University, and I always enjoyed hearing him talk about the Civil War. On the walls in his home was a Civil War gun collection, which was very impressive to this Quaker boy.

—Westside Park is just two blocks away. There we spent many a summer afternoon playing baseball.

—Just beyond the ball diamond is a bridge which crosses the White River. Under that bridge I smoked my first and last cigar. I can't remember anything which tasted so bad before or since.

—The alleys around the neighborhood were always fun. I slowly walked through one on the south side near the park, down Celia Avenue, and then back to the corner of Ethel and

Britain Avenues. This was the route of our "Little 500" bike race. It was never a scheduled activity, but when May would roll around and everyone was talking about the Indy 500, invariably someone would suggest a bike race around the neighborhood. I never won, but I always finished.

—Nichol's Grocery Store was just three blocks away. Here you could get all the candy you could eat in a day for just a quarter. For fifteen cents you could buy a big bottle of pop. Many summer hours were spent sitting on Nichol's steps, eating cheap candy and burping cola.

—Walking back toward my old house on Ethel Avenue I stopped at the main line of the old Nickel Plate Road, and remembered the time that my new bicycle wheel got caught in between the track and ties. It was a close call. I had beaten the train across, but my front bike wheel became lodged. I pulled and pushed with no success. The train was fast approaching and blowing its whistle, and so I panicked and began to run away. Then . . . I remembered my father's face. I went back and gave it one more adrenalin-charged tug and it came loose with micro seconds to spare!

As I recall, it was in the midst of this calamity that I promised God I would enter some form of religious service.

—My mother has often said that as a boy I was an accident waiting to happen. She's right. I could conduct week-long tours in the neighborhood of all the places Jim Newby has been hurt. Here I fell off my bike—ten stitches. Over there I fell on a pop bottle—six stitches. Just across the alley I fell from a tree—four stitches. When Ball Memorial Hospital knew I was in town, they added extra emergency room staff. Somehow I survived, and I have the scars to prove it.

Growing up as the son of a Quaker pastor made me an easy target for jokes and teasing about fighting. I can remember waiting up one night for my father to return home from a meeting so that I could talk to him about this pacifism business. "What if someone punches you first. Am I still not allowed to hit back?" It just didn't make sense to a young boy who was living in a peer culture of eye for eye and tooth for tooth.

I kept my father up late into the night debating with him about when and if fighting was ever okay. At one point, close to the end of our discussion, he said, out of frustration, "All right . . . if you are pinned to the ground and some bully is hitting you, you can try to get him off." That was as far as my father could go. He was, indeed, a true Quaker pacifist.

There was a boy, John, in my class at school. He was as obnoxious a kid as anyone has ever met, and who, I was sure, could even test the bounds of my father's Quaker demeanor. As I knew him then, this kid could make the most difficult and troublesome people in your life seem a joy to be with. One morning in the school hallway we passed, brushing each other's shoulders. For fifteen-year olds who did not enjoy one another's company anyway, this was all that was needed to begin an angry verbal exchange of, "Hey watch it," which escalated into, "You and me, after school, in the St. Mary's lot!" The challenge was made. St. Mary's was the Catholic Church located across the street from our school, and its parking lot was the long-standing traditional place for the settling of neighborhood differences.

Since this incident occurred early in the day; we had a long time to think about the upcoming fight. I can remember feeling scared, but I tried hard to act as if I knew what I was doing. *I didn't.* I had never really fought with anyone before—at least not in this way. But I was enjoying the newfound acceptability by my peers as a result of the challenge. The "Quaker boy" was defying his tradition, and in each class I was receiving verbal encouragement. I was quickly becoming the conduit for all of the angry feelings that others had toward John.

All day long I could not concentrate on my studies. The question of "How will I explain this to my parents?" occupied my mind. I wanted to keep all of the attention I was receiving, but I did not want the pain which was yet to come.

The bell rang marking the end of the school day. I walked out of my last class to my locker. As I slowly passed the sea of students on each side of me, I saw John straight ahead. I tried to avoid eye contact as we both moved closer to one another. Since our lockers were nearly side by side, there was no way to avoid a confrontation. "Hi Jim, see you tomorrow!" With that, John threw his books into his locker, and ran out of the building. I stood there dumb-founded. Had John forgotten about the fight? Was he giving up?

I remember the feeling of victory I felt as John ran away. It only lasted a few moments, however. Almost immediately I moved from feeling victorious to feeling sorry for John. He must have felt terribly humiliated. I didn't feel good about myself. I did not want to be known as a "tough" boy who made others back down from fights. If only John had known that I was as scared as he was. "John, if you are reading this, let's get together before another sunset. I challenge you to a cup of coffee and a heart-to-heart conversation. I'll buy."

There is an old neighborhood in each of us—a place where we were formed and which we helped to form. The only place where it has stayed the same since leaving is in one's mind, for we know that time cannot stand still. The houses now look smaller and are in need of repair, the streets seem more narrow, the trees larger, and the people older. But this is still home, and I could still claim it as "My Neighborhood."

In his book, *All I Really Need to Know I Learned in Kindergarten*, Robert Fulghum writes: "There are places we all come from—deep, rooty, common places—that make us who we are. And we disdain them or treat them lightly at our peril.

We turn our backs on them at the risk of self contempt. There is a sense in which we need to go home again—and can go home again. Not to recover home, no. But to sanctify memory."

All of life is sacramental. Whether this sacrament of God in one's life is experienced along the streets and alleys of one's old neighborhood or in an experience of worship in Westminster Abbey, it is the *reality* of the spiritual experience, not the form of the sacrament which is important. I have learned anew that the alleys, yards, and trees of my old neighborhood are a part of my very being. I am an Ethel Avenue, Muncie, Indiana boy, and I cannot deny that. Nor do I want to.

Being in touch with who we are helps us to understand *whose* we are. At root, the process of remembering as we experience pilgrimage, evokes a memory of a spiritual center, a holy place, an inner sanctuary, an "inner neighborhood" if you will, where we reconnect with the living God. It is, in the end, to this home that we long to return, and where, out of the chaos, we will be recognized, claimed, and loved as our authentic selves.

• • •

SPIRITUAL AUTOBIOGRAPHY

Every happening, great and small is a parable whereby God speaks to us, and the art of life is to get the message.
— MALCOLM MUGGERIDGE

As pilgrims on a journey, we can track our way through chaos by defining our path in terms of spiritual autobiography. For men, especially, *who* they are is often tied to *what* they do. In chaos, when the "what we do" has lost meaning, it is a small step to conclude that "who we are" is also meaningless. By tracking our lives spiritually we can enlarge our understanding of who we are, separating our worthiness as children of the Creator, from what we do in our professional lives of employment.

As we reflect on our life journey, we can discern those "awakening" or nodal moments which issued in an important change of direction. What were those moments? Who are the persons who moved us into new places of thought and spirituality? By asking the question, "How was God working in my life at that time?," an outline of our spiritual autobiography will emerge.

I can discern three distinct movements in my own life, each of which was precipitated by an "awakening" moment. In retrospect, I see my life, in spiritual terms, as a movement toward wholeness, which is a continuous process, day by day. I was born in 1949 in Minneapolis, Minnesota. My parents were Quakers, and, as already noted, my father was a Quaker pastor. The Newbys have a long tradition within the people called Quakers. The only slippage since the seventeenth century was when my great, great, great grandfather was "disowned" for marrying a Methodist. I found the disownment certificate in my grandfather's Bible on the day of his funeral. I now keep it framed and sitting atop the credenza in my study—a source of pride rather than derision. It reads: "Richard Ricks, having accomplished his marriage contrary to our discipline, and having been treated with on the occasion, and not manifesting a disposition to condemn his deviation, we therefore disown him from being a member of our religious society."

I am a Christian and a Quaker because I was born in North America as a Christian and a Quaker. I have no doubt that had I been born in Hindu India, I would be a Hindu. And so the first stage of my faith journey can be marked as *tradition centered*. It did not take me long to learn the uniqueness of this tradition. Throughout my schooling in Minneapolis and Muncie (where we moved in 1958), I was the *only* Quaker in my class.

A few summers ago while studying at Princeton Seminary, I was perusing some of the latest book releases in the campus bookstore. I saw a biography of James Dean, the film actor, and knowing that he grew up in Indiana, in a Quaker home, I quickly opened the book to learn what the author had said about the Quaker influence on Dean. The biographer began the chapter dealing with this subject in these words: "A Quaker is one who can take the pomp out of any circumstance." As one who loves parties and "pomp," I was disappointed in the author's observation. And yet, I understand the image.

In my high school class there was a boy named Junior South. Junior did not "fit in" with the rest of my high school class. Because he had been held back at least two grades, he was older than we were. His clothes were tattered, and he spoke in a peculiar Tennessee dialect. Junior entered Burris High School in the middle of the eleventh grade, and dropped out in the spring. It wasn't a surprise when he did so. After all, he really wasn't "one of us." The object of too many bad jokes and the product of a poor home situation, Junior joined the marines; he desperately needed to find a place where he was accepted and liked for who he was. And he loved his country. This was all that I knew about Junior South.

In the fall of 1966, the beginning of my senior year, Junior South was a distant memory. All summer long my friends and I had been busy with dances, parties, working on our cars, and hanging out at the Dairy Queen. Of course, there were lawns to mow and the odd jobs to do so that we could earn some gas money. For most of that summer, however, we worked harder at playing than we did at working. The Beach Boys modeled a style of life that we sought to emulate. No one ever asked, "Where's Junior?" No one really cared. I remember sitting in class when the news first began to circulate through the school. "Do you remember Junior South?" Vaguely. "He has been killed in Vietnam." It was as if someone had hit me in the stomach. Before this moment I had never known anyone near my age who had died. Sure, I didn't know him well. He was different, and he was older, and he talked funny . . . and now he was *dead*. Cause of death? The victim of small arms fire.

Junior South did something for me in death that he could not do in life. He made me pay attention to him. When the "Moving Wall" Vietnam War Memorial was brought to my hometown a few years ago, I went to the park to view it, and to remember. It was a solemn occasion as I joined people walking up and down the V-shaped monument looking for the names of friends and relatives . . . *and remembering*.

With the help of a veteran I found Junior's name on the wall. I traced it on a sheet of tissue paper, and I wept. I wept for the life of a young man I hardly knew, didn't want to know in life, but who in death made me pay attention to him, and to the tragedy that was occurring in a faraway country. The death of Junior was an "awakening moment" for me, and I have not been the same since. This experience was the impetus which helped to move me from a mere *tradition-centered* faith journey, to being *activist-centered*.

After graduation from high school in Muncie in 1967, I moved with my family to Wichita, Kansas, where my father became pastor of University Friends Meeting, and where I enrolled in Friends University. My Quaker faith took on new meaning as I began to understand the radical dimensions of Jesus' teachings, and the Quaker concerns for peace, equality, and simplicity provided a springboard for my own social activism.

My generation matured with the Beatles. Our high school years were filled with the innocence of "Love Me Do" and "Eight Days a Week," and our college years found us singing "Revolution" and "Give Peace a Chance." High school was fun, and if it were possible I could have majored in party. I certainly had enough credits. Beginning with the death of Junior South, however, I entered college with my innocent view of the world crumbling. More and more I was coming face-to-face with the realities of suffering and injustice. It was a serious time when many of my generation forgot how to laugh. Somehow laughter seemed out of place in a world of war and racial rioting. To save the world from its destructive course was difficult business, and we took our job very seriously.

Upon reflection, these years of lost innocence can be seen as a time of seduction. The baby-boomers born in the late forties and fifties actually believed that they could save the world. All that we needed to do was to . . .

    —end the war in Vietnam,
    —integrate schools and neighborhoods,
    —educate the poor, and
    —fund more Great Society programs.

This was the social agenda of my generation, and we thought that by the end of the month (it may take two months) we could save the world from its ruinous ways. Idealism was at its peak. Self-righteousness and a feeling of invincibility were the two fuels that kept us moving.

Much of the energy surrounding the idealism of this time was a good thing. I am grateful for the passion and intensity of concern for the poor, as well as the vivid picture of the reality of modern warfare. Social injustice and the inhumanity of war should not be lost on our generation, nor should the lessons of civil disobedience. What should be lost, however, is the righteous indignation that is not coupled with love, humility, and tenderness, and the starry-eyed idealism that leaves no room for an understanding of human frailty.

And so, I entered college with a lot of hair and a lot of hope, not unlike most of my generation. The passing years have thinned the hair, and the hope has been tempered by experience. The memories of those years are still vivid, and what occurred during that time is an important part of who I am, and who my generation is.

In 1969 I was married, and I began work in the evenings at a local hospital as a respiratory therapy technician. I also found myself listening to my father a lot more. I remember running home from college one noon (we just lived a block away), excited to tell my father about how I was planning to defy the college authorities by organizing a vigil for peace. My father was a strong believer in the peace movement during this time, joining me in several marches, and so I expected his full support. After listening carefully to my plans, he leaned back in his chair, put his hand on his chin, and said, "James, you must pick carefully on which crosses you will choose to die." It was important tempering advice for youthful activism.

I became a Quaker pastor after graduation in 1971. Although my major was in sociology, I felt that I could combine my concern for society with spirituality, and make a greater impact for social change from a position inside the church. The more I read in the area of theology, the more I realized the need for some more education. And then I met Elton Trueblood.

I shall never forget the impression Dr. Trueblood made upon me—then a young pastor from Central City, Nebraska— nor the topic that occupied our first conversation together. I was a guest in my parent's home in Kansas, and Elton was in Wichita to help with the inauguration of a new President at Friends University. This man, the most distinguished and important figure in American Quakerism, was dining with us, and my father made sure that I sat next to him. "James," Dr. Trueblood said to me, "I want you to preach on the 'holy conjunction' *and.*" His point was that the Christian life is a life of balance and conjunction—the combination of the clear head *and* the warm heart; the inner life of devotion *and* the outer life of service; the conservation of important traditions *and* the necessity to be open to new ideas. In the span of forty-five minutes over dinner, Elton Trueblood had initiated within me a course of thought which has continued to this day. At the time I was in the same condition as Walt Whitman, who said, "I was simmering, simmering, simmering. Emerson brought me to a boil." It was Elton Trueblood who brought me to a boil. He was the impetus for moving me from an *activist-centered* journey, to a journey that was centered in the *intellect.*

I became captivated by the pursuit of knowledge and the development of the intellect, which issued in further study at the Earlham School of Religion and Princeton Theological Seminary. "It is the vocation of Christians in every generation," wrote Elton Trueblood, "to outthink all opposition." I took this challenge seriously, and devoted myself to the search for the perfect reason.

And then my father died, and I have had to face a pattern of loss ever since. These combined losses have caused chaos, and have helped to move me to experience a *heart-centered* dimension of my journey, which has issued in writing this book. This new movement of the heart and experience was partially expressed in some words I wrote during a graduation exercise at Earlham College:

> In the cosmic theater of life, I have been pondering just how important all of this attention to academic excellence is. It is a question I raise each time I hear of a student suicide, or learn about a student selling his or her ethics down the river in order to secure a good grade. There is a lot of pressure in a good academic institution. The torch of knowledge is the center of worship.

And yet what is knowledge without the wonder of faith? It seems to me that learned information is of little use to the world if it is not coupled with the formation of the spirit. A good liberal arts college will try hard to keep spiritual growth and academic success balanced in the lives of their students. But deep down I believe that if push came to shove they would sacrifice their concern for spirituality on the altar of academic achievement.

The idolatry of reason is a big problem at good colleges, and is a bigger problem for the professors who live and die in the world of academia. I find that the wonder and mystery of spirituality can temper this academic disease and I am always impressed by learned persons who not only have a "clear head" of reason, but a "tender heart" as well. It is a difficult combination to keep in balance, but, I am convinced, it is this combination that will lead to human wholeness and spiritual maturity.

My journey has taken me through a number of stages: (1)*tradition*-centered, to (2) *activist*-centered, to (3) *intellect*-centered, to (4) *heart-* and *experience*-centered. Regardless of the center, I have learned to appreciate and understand the need for all of these different emphases.

The Apostle Paul writes about growing up in every way, into Christ, "from whom the whole body, joined and knit together . . . when each part is working properly, makes bodily growth and up builds itself in love" (Eph. 4:16). Although Paul is writing about the various parts of the community, this is also helpful advice for our personal journeys, for when we have a healthy understanding of our tradition, the need to make that tradition *live* today by being active in concerns for social justice, to be able to defend our faith journey intellectually, and to be sensitive to the concerns of the heart and experience the living God in the Now, we "grow up" in a wholistic way. This is not to say that my personal faith journey encompasses the whole, but it does seem to me that a wholistic journey will, at least, hold in tension the elements of tradition, activism, the intellect, and the heart which I have experienced. As with Elizabeth L., I can review my life and see how the separate pieces fit together and form a meaningful pattern. "One door has closed so another could open," she writes. "It makes sense." She concludes with her testimony on trust: "I have no control over whether or not the sun will rise tomorrow, nor can I control what the days, weeks, and years ahead will bring to me. What I can do is learn to trust God's pattern as it unfolds one day at a time" (*Listen to the Hunger*).

Trusting God's pattern as it unfolds one day at a time. Moving into a heart-centered, and experience-sensitive focus on one's journey, open to the movement of God in even the most minute circumstances of life, increases trust. Control, being in control and allowing others to control us, is out of the question. "Wanting to control other people, to make them live as we'd have them live," writes Karen Casey, makes the attainment of serenity impossible" (*Each Day a New Beginning*). When we are open, chaos can move us into the *heart*, where we are centered and serene. The dictionary defines serene or serenity as, "expressive of inward calm." Within the center of this inner calm we can live into the fullness of what it means to be a spiritually created being, secure in the expectation that all shall be well.

. . .

THE BACK ROADS OF THE SPIRIT

Wandering the back roads, where I am reborn
in serenity and laughter.
— JAMES KAVANAUGH

One way to venture into the center of the heart is on back roads. In this context, the "back roads" to which I refer are *stories*.

Stories and imagination are intrinsically linked, and as Ted Loder has written, "Imagination is at core, the dancing partner of faith. Rather than denying or escaping 'Reality,' imagination extends the boundaries of reality" (*Quaker Life*, November, 1992).

Jesus understood the power of story in extending the boundaries of reality, and in intensifying the experience of pilgrimage. Every time Jesus spoke to the crowds, he did so in parables. Paragraph after paragraph throughout the Gospels begins, "Another parable he put before them." In the Gospel of Matthew we read, "Indeed he said nothing to them without a parable" (Matt. 13:34). In calculating the character of the canon, we discover that over half of both Testaments are stories.

Stories can often provide the medium to express our deepest feelings—feelings which could not find adequate expression without them. For example, from *Winnie the Pooh* . . .

> Piglet sidled up to Pooh from behind. "Pooh," he whispered.
> "Yes, Piglet?"
> "Nothing," said Piglet, taking Pooh's paw,
> "I just wanted to be sure of you."

Or, from *Charlotte's Web* . . .

> Wilbur blushed. "But I'm not terrific, Charlotte. I'm just about average for a pig."
> "You're terrific as far as I am concerned," replied Charlotte, "and that's what counts. You're my best friend, and I think you're sensational."

Stories nudge us into our imaginations and the world of dreams, and consequently, onto the unmarked back roads of the spirit. It is to take our experience of pilgrimage and quest for spiritual intimacy beyond the well-marked interstate highway of legalisms and pronouncements on the "shoulds" and "oughts" of religion, and enter a realm of mystery where each of us is a unique story which is continuously unfolding.

For those looking for hard and fast answers to the most important *why* questions of life, you will not find them within the storytelling genre. You will find, instead, paradox and mystery, which, in the quest for spiritual intimacy, are central. To accept God's invitation to wander the back roads of the spirit, is to come to that place in one's pilgrimage when you recognize that . . .

> *imagination* is stronger than knowledge . . .
> *myth* is more potent than history . . .
> *dreams* are more powerful than facts . . .
> *hope* always triumphs over experience . . .
> *laughter* is the only cure for grief . . . and
> *love* is stronger than death.
> — ROBERT FULGHUM, *The Storyteller's Creed*

Wandering the back roads of the spirit. It is a rather poetic way of saying that there is more to our experience of pilgrimage than we can ever know through one-dimensional "just the facts," kind of living. Through the medium of stories we can enter new dimensions of imagination, myth, dreams, hope, laughter, and love, all of which enrich our pilgrimage and help to make our chaos sacred.

. . .

AND . . . IN THE END . . . THERE IS NO END . . .

Love can consign us to hell or to paradise, but it will always take us somewhere. We simply have to accept it, because it is what nourishes our existence. If we reject it, we die of hunger. . . .
The moment we begin to seek love, love begins to seek us.
And to save us.
— PAULO COELHO

There are places throughout our pilgrimage where we return again and again for the memories of healing which took place there. These could include a church sanctuary, a view from the top of a hill or mountain, a favorite stretch of beach, or a path through the woods. For me, it is the "Battleground Park" in Greensboro, North Carolina. It was here that I would walk or run daily, praying, talking to myself, or turning something over and over in my heart and mind. It was here that I would come to cry or to yell, relieving the inner pain which could, at times, immobilize me.

Around this three-mile trek in the middle of suburban sprawl, the path passes by a cemetery, and for at least a half-mile each day I was confronted with the reality of my own mortal demise. Day after day I would look out on the remains of those who had passed before me—lives which had been similar to my own in that they all experienced joy and pain; victory and defeat, love and fear. And, I knew as I passed, that the day would come in my own earthly pilgrimage when I would join the lifeless forms with the name, JAMES R. NEWBY etched into a piece of granite.

Each time I walked or ran by this sea of tombstones, the words of the poet, John Greenleaf Whittier, would always come to mind—words which I so grew to love that they became imprinted upon my heart:

> Alas for him who never sees
> The stars shine through the cypress trees.
> Who hopeless lays his dead away,
> Nor looks to see the breaking day
> Across the mournful marbles play.
> Who hath not learned in hours of faith
> The truth that time and sense have known,
> That life is ever lord of death,
> And love can never lose its own.

Life, I am convinced, is a continuum. I reach this conclusion through no amount of scientific rigor or naive hopefulness. It is something I *feel*, and in which I have *faith*. Love is the constant, and when this mortal bag of bones and flesh is put to rest for the last time, the love will continue. As spirit, whether I am invited to come back into this world through the miracle of reincarnation, or continue to grow in the next world, I know that the love I have experienced and expressed will be constant. "Love can never lose its own," wrote the poet—the love found in *passion* for life; the *pain* we experience; the *prayers* with which we search the world of spirit; the *paradoxes* in which we live, and the spiritual *pilgrimage* where the meaning of life can be discovered. And because of this *love*, our quest for spiritual intimacy will always be in process . . .

EPILOGUE

The Afterglow

There is no fear in love, but perfect love casts out fear.
— 1 JOHN 4:18

We are never *totally* out of chaos, and we are never *totally* in order. Our experiences throughout life will cause us to fluctuate from one emphasis to the other, but there are no clear, distinct lines of separation between the two. The transformation out of chaos is forever unfolding. It is a continuous process, preparing us for the next step of growth in self-awareness. And, I believe, self-awareness and God awareness are one and the same.

This said, there are respites from chaos, which I refer to as *the afterglow*. Afterglow is a term which has been used primarily to describe the experience immediately following sexual intercourse, and a comparison between the sexual act and chaos could be made. After all, it is a thin line which separates the feelings of intense spirituality and intense sensuality, thus making the term *afterglow* appropriate here.

The afterglow provides us time and space to reflect on lessons learned and meditate on the experiences through which we have recently traveled. I am now in such an afterglow time, writing, reflecting, and meditating. As I have lived into recovering passion, processing pain, exploring prayer, dancing with paradox, and experiencing pilgrimage—clarity in my spiritual quest has emerged. Comforted by the words I heard on a North Carolina beach three years ago, "Everything is going to be all right," I realize that being "all right" does *not* mean finding my own personal comfort zone, and certainly not falling back into familiar patterns which life offered before the chaos. This would be an impossible spiritual task, even if attempted. What the "all right" has come to mean for me is a redirection of energy, whereby the spiritual quest has become central. I hold the words of John close to my heart: "There is no fear in love, but perfect love casts out fear" (1 John 4:18). This "perfect love" is at one end of life's continuum, while codependency, spiritually deadening patterns of behavior, such as control and power over others, guilt, and fear, reside at the other end. It is wrong to claim that I have reached the "perfect love," professed by John, but it is equally wrong to say it is unachievable. Out of my chaos, which broke so many of the deadening patterns of the past, I can say that the *focus of intent* on perfect love is within me, and it is within us all.

Some of the marks of such perfect love are *justice* for everyone; *peace*, both inner and between individuals and nations; *equality* between the races, sexes, and those of different sexual orientation; *community*, wherein we recognize our responsibility for one another; *integrity*, by which we practice honesty, openness and speak truth to all; *simplicity* in living, whereby the barriers of materialism which obstruct growth in the spirit can be eliminated, and an ever growing *sensitivity* of connection with the entire created order. Perfect love, at the very least, embodies these noble possibilities within the creation.

Most of the time I do not realize these possibilities. I can practice injustice with the best of them, and anger can cause rifts between me and others. I can also shade the truth and trample upon the created order. I know how to be cruel. Whenever I find myself practicing these less than loving behaviors, I realize, again, that God is not yet done with me. The quest into spiritual intimacy continues. I am not discouraged by such backsliding, but I am reminded of my own humanity and the need to refocus my intent. There is no end to the times we can reset our "perfect love" focus. God is a God of new beginnings, and of these new beginnings there is no end. And even in the midst of uncertainty and pain, we encounter the words of Julian of Norwich, which rise just over the horizon . . .

And all shall be well . . .
And all shall be well . . .
And all manner of things shall be well . . .

BIBLIOGRAPHY

Arendt, Hannah. *The Life of the Mind*, Vol. 1. *Thinking*. New York: Harcourt, Brace, Jovanovich, 1971–77.

Augustine, Saint. *The City of God*. New York: Hafner Publishing Co., 1948.

———. *The Confessions of Saint Augustine*. New York: Modern Library, 1949.

Barclay, Robert. *The Apology*. Philadelphia, 1908.

Beattie, Melody. *Codependent No More*. San Francisco: Harper Collins, 1987.

———. *The Language of Letting Go*. San Francisco: Harper Collins, 1990.

Bianco, Williams Margery. *The Velveteen Rabbit*. Garden City, New York: Doubleday, 1982.

Borg, Marcus. *Meeting Jesus Again for the First Time*. San Francisco: Harper Collins, 1994.

Boulding, Kenneth. *There Is a Spirit: The Nayler Sonnets*. New York: Fellowship Publications, 1945.

Casey, Karen. *Each Day a New Beginning*. San Francisco: Harper Collins, 1982.

Chase, Mary. *Harvey: Comedy in Three Acts*. New York: Dramatists Play Service, 1944.

Coelho, Paulo. *By the River Piedra I Sat Down and Wept*. San Francisco: Harper Collins, 1996.

Donne, John. *Devotions*. Cambridge, England: The University Press, 1923.

Fulghum, Robert. *All I Really Need to Know I Learned in Kindergarten*. New York: Villard Books, 1988.

Hart, Moss. *Act One*. New York: Random House, 1959.

Hoff, Ben. *The Tao of Pooh*. New York: E. P. Dutton, 1982.

Jones, Rufus. *The Luminous Trail*. New York: Macmillan, 1947.

Kavanaugh, James. *Will You Be My Friend?* San Francisco: Harper and Row, 1984.

Kazantzakis, Nikos. *Zorba the Greek.* New York: Simon and Schuster, 1953.

Keen, Sam. *Fire in the Belly.* New York: Bantam Books, 1991.

———. *Hymns to an Unknown God.* New York: Bantam Books, 1994.

———. *To a Dancing God.* New York: Harper and Row, 1970.

Kelly, Thomas. *A Testament of Devotion.* New York: Harper and Brothers, 1941.

Kierkegaard, Søren. *Journals.* London: Oxford University Press, 1938.

Kornfield, Jack. *A Path with Heart.* New York: Bantam Books, 1993.

L., Elizabeth. *Listen to the Hunger.* San Francisco: Harper Collins, 1987.

Marshall, Catherine. *A Man Called Peter.* New York: McGraw-Hill, 1951.

Mansfield, Katherine. *Journal.* Ed. J. Middleton Murry. New York: Alfred A. Knopf, 1933.

Merton, Thomas. *Love and Living.* Ed. N. B. Stone and P. Hart. New York: Bantam Books, 1979.

Milne, A. A. *Winnie the Pooh.* New York: E. P. Dutton and Co., 1926.

Moore, Thomas. *Care of the Soul.* New York: Harper Collins, 1992.

Muggeridge, Malcolm. *A Twentieth-Century Testimony.* Nashville: Thomas Nelson,1978.

Nakken, Craig. *The Addictive Personality.* San Francisco: Harper Collins, 1988.

Nayler, James. *See* Boulding, Kenneth

Penington, Mary. *Experiences in the Life of Mary Penington.* London: Headley Brothers, 1911.

Penn, William. *The Rise and Progress of the People Called Quakers.* Richmond, Ind.: Friends United Press, 1977.

———. *Fruits of Solitude.* London: Headley Brothers, 1905.

Quaker Life. Mar. 1991; Nov. 1992; June 1993; Dec. 1993.

Radner, Gilda. *It's Always Something.* New York: Simon and Schuster, 1989.

Schaeffer, Brenda. *Is It Love or Is It Addiction.* San Francisco: Harper Collins, 1987.

Schweitzer-Mordecai, Ruth. *Spiritual Freedom.* San Francisco: Harper Collins,1991.

Toffler, Alvin. *Future Shock.* New York: Random House, 1970.

Walsch, Neale Donald. *Conversations with God, Book 1.* New York: G. P. Putnam's Sons, 1995.

White, E. B. *Charlotte's Web.* New York: Harper Collins, 1980.

Whittier, Greenleaf John. *The Complete Poetical Works of . . .* Boston/New York: Houghton Mifflin and Company, 1904.

Woolman, John. *The Journal and Major Essays of John Woolman.* Ed. Amelia Mott Gummere. New York: Macmillan, 1922.